COMPENDIUM

Spiritual Care through Muslim Ethnographic Stories

The Absent Student: The Bird

Volume 4

Dr. Yunus Kumek

Sage Chronicle ^λ
publishing house

Cover image: Unsplash.com

Sage Chronicle $^{\lambda}$
publishing house

www.sagechronicle.org
3380 Sheridan Drive, #240
New York 14226
contact@sagechronicle.org

PREFACE

This book brings into our contemporary life important Muslim teachings in a one-page story format. Each story has the first paragraph as the story and the second paragraph as the meanings and interpretations of the practice. The stories in the book aim to use contemporary life encounters with the meanings and interpretations in Islamic practice. These stories have been compiled and contemporized from ethnographic field work in different Sufi communities of New York, Boston, Pittsburgh, Chicago, Toronto, Istanbul, and Cairo.

The book uses a simple transliteration scheme from the original language of Arabic without going to the details of academic transliteration scheme. When there are names or referrals to God then the words are capitalized such as the Divine. The abbreviation used for the Prophet Muhammad is the Prophet. The footnotes with numbered superscripts give the immediate relevant information for the unfamiliar English reader. The endnotes with lettered superscripts give the information for the reader who is familiar with the teachings and readings in Sufism. The references with numbered and parenthesis superscripts allude to the notions in practice as some examples of these practices in the literature. The suggested readings are examples of some classical and contemporary work about the topic for interested readers. The glossary and index in the book can hopefully make it easier for general readers of English.

The short stories and anecdotes in this book can bring important and practical aspects of these teachings in our practical life. This book can be valuable for different level readers such as the Muslims, Christians, Jews, Buddhists, Hindus, and people who especially value spirituality and experiential knowledge and believe the mysteries of life beyond the seen and human control. Regardless of different naming of the deity as Allah, God, Adonai, or the notions of Nirvana or Samadhi, in this book, one can realize the similarity of common and intersecting points of spirituality or religious experience among different traditions.

The word "Sufi" or character of "Sufi" does not imply a group or sect in this case, but used to depict a self-reflective personality or a character trying to have a spiritual Muslim care in daily practices. So, each time you see the Sufi character, you can imagine and replace it with a "Muslim". It was also easy for me especially for Western audience just to denote everything as one character as Muslim without changing genders and trying to find 500 different Muslim gender names in more than 500 stories.

This book can be a valuable supplementary text in the disciplines of psychology, counseling, anthropology, philosophy, and religion.

Yunus Kumek, PhD
Lecturer in Muslim Ministry
Harvard Divinity School
Fall 2022

CONTENTS

COMPENDIUM

Spiritual Care through Muslim Ethnographic Stories

The Absent Student: The Bird

1.   Rewards & End Results

There was once a Sufi who had children. Each time they read the Qur'an, they would report their progress to their father and then expect a reward from the Sufi. The Sufi would then purchase toys for them. There was also a wise-fool who would read the Qur'an at the mosque. Each time he read the Qur'an, he would also visit the Sufi, mention how much he had read, and expect a reward. The Sufi would then give him several dollars. The Sufi then considered both instances and thought to himself, "The importance of rewards, encouragement, and the need for Heaven in the afterlife . . .

IN PRACTICE

It is essential to make every effort to please Allah ﷻ. Each individual's relationship with Allah ﷻ is unique. It is normal to feel inspired and motivated by the outcome. This outcome could be a toy, a few dollars, or an eternity in heaven. Yet, the highest and most noble of these outcomes is Allah ﷻ's Pleasure.

2.   The Love of the Prophet

One day, the Sufi attended a lecture on Prophetic adoration. He was glad he attended to witness the speaker's profound devotion to the Prophet. The Sufi then said to himself, "I hope we can embody the genuine love for Rasulullah ﷺ, but it must be genuine."

In practice

Rasulullah ﷺ Muhammad is the finest pearl and diamond among all humans in terms of his actions and personality. When one examines the life of Rasulullah ﷺ in depth, one realizes that he was the epitome of compassion, gentleness, patience, and serenity. Nonetheless, his example of anger control and a just, fair personality exemplifies a person who lived a perfect human life. The humanity of this perfect role model demonstrates to the followers how well the Divine Teachings can be applied to the lives of all humans.

Discussion Questions

- ▶ What in particular do you love about Rasulullah ﷺ Muhammad, or any of the prophets?
- ▶ In what ways do you try to model the behaviors and attitudes of Muhammad and the other prophets in your life?

3.   Realities, Definitions and Dresses

There once was a Sufi who studied psychology. She was contemplating the definitions of human psychological states. As expected in each discipline, there were a large number of technical and convoluted terms. Yet, the Sufi said to herself, "Our definitions and terms in each discipline are comparable to the clothing we wear. Although the dress may appear to be a good fit, it may not accurately represent the wearer."

In practice

There are various disciplines and methods, such as psychology, that contribute to our understandings of ourselves. Yet, sometimes a discipline's technical term for the classification of a person, derived after much effort, may not accurately represent the inner mind and emotional renderings of a person in its true reality and purpose. In some instances, these terms can be a diversion that separates the individual from their true self. Therefore, for the people of the heart (ahlullah), mere mental knowledge is invalid unless confirmed by experience in accordance with the Qur'an and *sunnah*,[1] applications of Quranic teachings by Rasulullah . Muhammad.

---

1. Practices and applications of teachings of the Qurān by Rasulullah ﷺ Muhammad.

4.   Love On the Way

There were two Sufis-a husband and a wife. One day, the Sufi husband suffered an injury to a limb. The Sufi wife delivered a lengthy lecture on how he does not take proper care of himself. A week later, the Sufi wife received a cut on the exact same limb as her Sufi husband. The Sufi wife stated, "Perhaps it is because of my less than favorable thoughts about my husband."

IN PRACTICE

When people are close to Allah ﷻ, Allah ﷻ will sometimes send them small warnings with love, kindness, and concern so they can correct their behavior. As in the preceding story, it is anticipated that these pleasant warnings will encourage a person to engage in self-reflection.

Discussion Questions

- ► Have you ever noticed a loving reminder being sent when your attitude or behavior needed adjustment?
- ► Are you grateful and receptive when you receive correction?
- ► How can we become more grateful for correction from others, and use it to improve ourselves, our relationships, and our lives?
- ► How can we learn to take criticism from others in stride, and not have a negative reaction to it, internally or externally?
- ► How can we learn to be less critical of others?

5. External Evil Revisited

The Sufi was on the road. She once more felt the presence of evil that had previously visited her. She said to herself, "I believed I had overcome this evil." It arrived again. She immediately recited her litany of protection prayers.

IN PRACTICE

As long as we inhabit a world containing both evil and good, there will always be a fluctuation between the two. This evil can originate from the individual's own self. It can also originate externally. Regardless, a person should always be prepared to seek refuge in Allah ﷻ with the litany of prayers in response to ominous events.

6.   Owner's Manual

The Sufi purchased a new machine from Amazon one day. He was overjoyed and carefully reading the manual as he assembled the item. While working diligently and carefully, he was also considering the concept of a human manual. Then he thought to himself, "Yes, it is the Qur'an that Allah ﷻ sent."

IN PRACTICE

With the Quran, Allah ﷻ teaches us our own realities. In common speech, the Qur'an is the manual for humans. If a person attempts to figure out how to use a simple machine without a manual, he or she may spend hours and still not fully comprehend its operation. In contrast, if a person reads the manual with a little bit of effort, he or she will be able to comprehend and use this machine step by step. If there are problems, one can always refer to the manual to determine the issues and their solutions. Similarly, the Qur'an and all prophetic teachingsxlii are the full, comprehensive, and exhaustive manual for the individual. The individual constantly interacts with them in order to comprehend their true selves and pupose in this brief lifetime. If a person acts in accordance with self-absorbed dispositions, he or she will waste this brief life on delusions. As long as they are evaluated in accordance with the principles and guidelines of these scriptural and prophetic teachings[i], all of these discoveries have genuine value[ii].

7.   The Dedication of the Book and the News

The Sufi wrote a book one day. She dedicated it to one of her old friends who resided in a foreign nation. She submitted the manuscript to be published. The following day, she received a text message informing her that her friend had been killed in a bicycle accident. The Sufi changed the book dedication to include the date and added a note that read, "just received a text that he died in a bicycle accident today."

In practice

Constantly remembering the reality of death is essential. Death is a common topic that should be realized and practiced by learners of all ages and skill levels. In this sense, death is not evil, but rather the individual's desired return to Allah ﷻ.

8.   Being Present and Not Remembering the Past

The Sufi pondered one day that being fully present in the present should require forgetting the past. The Sufi could not recall what she wrote and mused on yesterday. She thought to herself, "Perhaps I am now fully present."

In practice

Being present is essential. Nonetheless, planning for the future and the afterlife is the primary purpose of life. The individual on the path toward Allah ﷻ is a successful businessperson on the spiritual path. The person's ultimate objective is the afterlife. On the spiritual journeys of strengthening the heart, mind, and body, a person receives immediate benefits in this world.

9.   The Health of Faith & Practice

One day, the Sufi reflected on the difficulty of maintaining one's *iman*, faith, and practice as one advances in life and engages in various worldly pursuits. He said to himself, "Despite your efforts, your *iman* could become infected at any time. Constantly contracting these diseases is disgusting, and one must exert effort in order to keep it clean."

In practice

Yes, maintaining a healthy state of iman, faith, and practice is extremely difficult. With the favor and power of Allah ﷻ, nothing is impossible. However, if one can recognize disgust as a symptom of these spiritual diseases, this is a positive sign. The individual is vigilant and self-aware of impending diseases. The next step is to make an effort to purge them through *istigfar,* asking for forgiveness, and *ibadah,* engaging in worship.

10. Effect of Clothes

The Sufi went for a walk in the rain one day. He arrived at the mosque drenched in rain. He discovered pants and a shirt. He donned them himself. His pants and shirt were small and extremely snug. He experienced spiritual constriction and a headache. He thought to himself, "This may be the result of the clothing."

IN PRACTICE

What a person wears has an effect on his or her spirituality. The term 'modesty' can reflect this similar concept found in religious dress codes. Sometimes, wearing a tight garment, a colorful dress, a cap, a turban, a headscarf, or a long dress can have a negative or positive spiritual effect on the individual. When a person makes the intention to emulate a role model in their dress, such as the Virgin Mary or Rasulullah ﷺ Muhammad, Allah ﷻ rewards them and bestows spiritual empowerment upon them.

Discussion Questions

- ▶ What do you base your decisions on for choosing your clothing each day?
- ▶ Do you notice a difference in the way you feel and behave based on what type of clothing you are wearing?
- ▶ What type of clothing do you like to wear when you are planning to pray or meditate and spend time with Allah ﷻ? What is it about that kind of clothing that makes you choose it for this occasion? How does it make you feel?

11. Fine Lines of *Iman*

There was once a Sufi whom everyone adored. They adored the Sufi teachings she imparted. The Sufi said to herself one day, "Does Allah ﷻ not reward? I desire others to admire my efforts of teaching them about authentic practices, yet I hope it is an opportunity to be closer to Allah ﷻ."

IN PRACTICE

Occasionally, the arrogance of piety, religiosity, or the conceit of teaching others about Allah ﷻ can cause a person to stray from the path. Yes, it is valuable and encouraging to share what one finds valuable with others. In doing so, one can please Allah ﷻ but it is not the only way.

12. Worldly & Spiritual-Seeming Achievements & Fatalities

One day, the Sufi was evaluating her life experiences. She was attempting to replay the events in her mind. There were instances of apparent worldly and spiritual accomplishments. She thought to herself, "Based on my life, it appears that I have suffered fatal spiritual crashes. When I lost sight of my true objective, the ends became entangled in false means.

IN PRACTICE

Everything and anything can serve as a test or trial. *Tayaqquz,* or vigilance with full and humbling refuge in Allah ﷻ, is the key to safety precautions.

13. Two Crazy-Fools

Two crazy-fools used to frequent the mosque to pray and hang out. One was elderly while the other was young. The older one used to become enraged whenever the younger one entered the mosque, telling him, "Wash yourself (wudhu) before entering the mosque." Come then and pray." The younger fool used to be displeased by this. However, out of respect for the elder, he would perform wudhu and then begin praying. As this continued for some time, the younger individual stopped attending the mosque to avoid seeing the older man. One day, the *imam* led the congregation in prayer. During the prayer, the cell phone of the older fool started to ring. After the prayer, the *imam* delivered a lengthy lecture about turning off cell phones during the prayer. The older fool was insulted and stopped attending the mosque.

In practice

It is essential to communicate without offending the recipient. Although the individual may be correct, the wrong way of delivering the information can sometimes cause more harm than not delivering the correct information. Although difficult, one should train themselves to see things from both perspectives. In addition, the preceding narrative illustrates the attribute of Allah ﷻ that is Just. If we offend others, someone will likely offend us as well.

14.   Theoretical Physicist Sufi and Mind Wanderings

There was a quantum physicist who was also a Sufi. She reflected on her life while pursuing a PhD in theoretical physics. She used to become so engrossed in a problem that she could not escape for hours. As she progressed in her spirituality, she realized that mind wanderings without guidelines can sometimes be fruitless.

She applied this spirituality-related concept to her theoretical physics-related mental travels. Now, her problem-solving endeavors related to the journeys of quantum physics were producing more effective outcomes.

IN PRACTICE

It is essential to adhere to the guidelines. The Qur'an and the teachings of the Prophet Muhammad[2] can serve as such guidelines. It is important to engage in self-reflection, critical thinking, and experiential journeys so long as these guidelines are adhered to, preferably in the company of a competent and trustworthy instructor. On another note, one can observe in practice how science teachings can be related to spiritual teachings.

---

2. Hadith and Sunnah.

15.   Not Dying After Death

The Sufi wondered one day, "How can I not die after my physical death?" She responded with "*Dua.*"

IN PRACTICE

It is necessary to pray in order to survive after death. Abraham is one of the examples of Rasulullah ﷺ in this case. In the Qur'an, it is stated that he prays to Allah ﷻ so that he will be remembered as a good person and produce virtuous children. As we can see, his prayers are accepted, his legacy lives on, and his teachings are fondly remembered.

16. The Crazy-Fool and the Cleaner in the Mosque

The Sufi was sitting in the mosque when the crazy-fool arrived one day. The Sufi was the crazy-fool's only friend. The madman was angry with everyone, including his own relatives. As usual, the Sufi offered the crazy-fool some delicious treats and coffee, but he acted very formally and remained silent. Then, the mosque's cleaner entered. His name, Habib, translates to "the lover." Habib was a nice and quiet man, but he did not think highly of the crazy-fool. The idiot began conversing with Habib about the weather and life. The crazy-fool was speaking incessantly. Habib had to return to his duties cleaning the mosque. He was unable to do so because the madman was shouting and ranting about people and life without pausing. The Sufi observed this and thought to himself, "This is why I am behaving formally."

IN PRACTICE

In order to know how to approach different individuals, it is crucial to attempt to comprehend their individual personalities and needs. A person can assist another in numerous ways without revealing their weaknesses. The Sufi was aware of the crazy-fool. To prevent himself from being humiliated, he pretended to act formally. Nonetheless, he treated him with respect. Sufi was his sole companion in life. Allah ﷻ has granted genuine Sufis the ability to be good friends with everyone, including those who are disliked or frightening. There are accounts of Sufis being friends with both snakes and lions.

17. The Realities and Short-Lifed Mind and Experiential Renderings

One day, the Sufi attended a gathering where the emphasis was on experience and spiritual enlightenment, with little mention of Qur'anic and Sunnah guidelines. They appeared to discredit the scriptural knowledge. The Sufis later attended a gathering where the emphasis was on the mind rather than experience and genuine sincerity exemplified by *adab*. They appear to discredit experience. The Sufi reflected, "The journey is so challenging. It is always essential to maintain equilibrium."

In practice

One may emphasize statements such as "If my heart is good and pure, I do not need to follow and practice the authentic Qur'an." On the other hand, others may not value an individual's inner dispositions, but rather their external qualities. However, the key is to balance the internal and external. This equilibrium can be revealed when a person follows and practices the five daily prayers and other essential components of the practice. However, they must also attempt to internalize the deeper meanings of these practices.

18.   The Realities, our Weaknesses and our Short Life

The Sufi received bad news regarding her work one day. Later that day, she learned that her mother had been admitted to the hospital after possibly suffering a stroke. Then, she became ill. She thought to herself, "We are so frail and our lives are so brief. "There is no refuge other than in Allah ﷻ."

IN PRACTICE

The key is to turn to Allah ﷻ in both times of ease and difficulty. In times of distress, our weak willpower prevents us from turning to Allah ﷻ. Nevertheless, there is never any other solution, whether in need or not, than to turn to Allah ﷻ.

19.   The Angels and their Appearance

One day, one of the revered and renowned Sufi teachers embarked on a pilgrimage. During his travels, he observed a woman searching through a garbage can for food. The Sufi instructor questioned what she was doing. She stated that she was seeking food for her children. The Sufi teacher gave her all of his money and food, then returned home after days of traveling. After the pilgrimage season concluded, the pilgrims began returning to their homes. They all came to the teacher's classroom to discuss his emotional sermon during the pilgrimage. Everyone was in tears. The Sufi instructor did not comprehend and did not respond to anyone. He prayed and asked Allah to reveal the situation to him. He then slept. In his dream, he was told that Allah was so pleased with his action that an angel accompanied him on pilgrimage and delivered a sermon. The acceptance of everyone's pilgrimage was due to his sincere action.

In practice

A simple and sincere deed can strengthen a person's relationship with Allah ﷻ. The key to one's relationship with Allah ﷻ may not be the quantity of one's worship, but his or her intense sincerity.

20. Complaints & Lack of Appreciation

There was a Sufi whose wife frequently lodged complaints against him. His wife consistently claimed that the Sufi did nothing around the house. She is always the one doing everything. The Sufi would inquire, "What do you want me to do? Please provide specific details." His wife would provide a "to-do" list, which the Sufi would complete to the best of his ability. His wife was previously happy. After some time, the Sufi's wife began to repeat herself. The Sufi requested the explicit "to-do list" once more. Then, she was once again happy. The cycle persisted.

In practice

Complaints add no value and increase everyone's resentment. In familial, professional, and other relationships, some individuals may perform more work than others. This may be true. On the other hand, those who do more work should not act as "the savior," while those who do less work should express their appreciation for the hard workers and try to contribute as much as possible despite the other party's complaints. Establishing relationships and performing deeds that please Allah ﷻ can reduce or eliminate resentment when others do not recognize a person's efforts.

21. Eschatology, Necessary and Unnecessary Engagements

There was a Sufi who was eating with his companions. Her friends began a discussion about eschatological cases and the possibilities surrounding the end of the world. Her friends were enthusiastic about the subject, but not the Sufi. The Sufi said to herself, "Every learning endeavor must have a worthy objective. The mere desire to acquire knowledge for no particular reason can induce fear, anxiety, and distraction."

In practice

It is essential to learn and participate in any conversation or lecture with a clear purpose and objective. Simply chatting or loitering may cause a person's mind to wander and become distracted. Rasulullah ﷺ requested protection from knowledge that did not benefit the individual [51]. On the other hand, it is possible to study and investigate eschatology with intent and purpose. These include, for instance, normalizing the occurrences and changes in societies through foretold prophetic miracles, and possibly using these avenues to explain to people that changes in our lives or societies are not random, but rather are under Allah ﷻ' s control and knowledge.

22.   Real Teachers Don't Judge

A Sufi teacher was so gentle, kind, and forgiving of people's errors. Another Sufi used to learn a great deal from this teacher. Yet, he continued to make mistakes with regard to not judging others and being as kind and gentle as his teacher. The Sufi said to himself, "I strive to be like my teacher, despite the difficulty."

IN PRACTICE

As humans, we make mistakes. All the Prophets possessed this quality as authentic teachers. Rasulullah ﷺ Muhammad was a very kind and gentle teacher who consistently implemented this gentleness and kindness in human relations, whereas we have a tendency to rush to judgment in human relationships. This is the most significant distinction between ordinary spiritual people and the highest role models. However, we should all strive to be like our role models.

23.   Headache, Arrogance & Prostration

The Sufi had a severe headache one day. He was at a loss for what to do. He said, "Let me pray." He began praying, and each time he placed his head on the ground in prostration, he felt so good, his headache was relieved, and he remained with his head on the ground for a considerable amount of time. He told himself, "This headache is probably due to my arrogance." Allah ﷻ desires that I humble myself through prostration in order to alleviate this arrogant headache."

In practice

It is essential to establish a connection between external and internal diseases. Every occurrence in a person's life is connected to his or her internal engagement. With Allah ﷻ's assistance, it can be simple to treat both internal and external diseases if a person is self-aware.

24. Silence, Smile & Sakina

There was a Sufi who desired eternal *sakina,* or Allah's peace and tranquility. She used to perpetually smile and remain silent. If she needed to speak, she would do so in a few words with a very pleasant and soft voice and tone. Then she would observe silence and smile, as this was the majority of her engagement. She always experienced *sakina,* a blessing from Allah .

IN PRACTICE

Harsh and unruly speech and behavior can destroy one's *iman,* or faith. As granted by Allah, the flavor of this honey is *sakina,* tranquility, peace, and serenity. Rasulullah Muhammad exemplified this characteristic. He used to smile frequently and speak little. When he spoke, he utilized few words with profound and wise meanings[iii]. One of our problems today is that we cannot know when to stop talking.

25.   Submission & the Sufi

One day, the Sufi desired to be in a position to benefit humanity. Then, he immediately reined in his emotions and thoughts and exclaimed, "Astagfirullah, Oh Allah ﷻ!, Oh Allah ﷻ, I am pleased with whatever You desire. If You are unhappy with it, please do not give it to me. You are my Determinant. I completely submit to You."

IN PRACTICE

There are various spiritual states and levels. Two of them are reliance and submission, terms with similar but distinct meanings. Reliance[exlv] is employing necessary means and relying on Allah ﷻ for the results of these means. In addition to the requirements of Reliance[iv], submission[v] is not desiring or asking for anything other than to submit oneself to the One Who is the All-Knower and Holder of Good.

26. Marriage Proposal and the Sufi

There was a Sufi who was unmarried. He saw a girl by chance and fell in love with her. Then, after many days and weeks of experiencing the agony of love, he attempted to determine whether she was interested in getting married. Then, arrangements were made to meet with her. As soon as he saw her, the Sufi asked, "Would you please marry me? I love you so much." She responded with "Yes." The Sufi began to jump up and down due to his happiness. The girl stated that she has a sister who is more beautiful than herself. The Sufi exclaimed, "Are you joking? Where? The girl stated, "There she is." The Sufi turned away and died instantly. The girl stated, "A true lover never takes his eyes off his beloved for even a moment."

In practice

We claim to love Allah ﷻ. Yet, our attention shifts as we anticipate benefit from others. When we neglect *La ilaha illa Allah,* we are preparing for our spiritual demise.

27. Coming Back to Earth and Social Problems

There was a Sufi who enjoyed spending time alone with Allah ﷻ. She realized one day that she needed to return to earthly realities in order to address social issues and assist people. *Alhamdulillah,* if it pleased Allah ﷻ, I would do it.

In practice

Everything's goal and purpose is to please Allah ﷻ. Consequently, worshiping in solitude is performed to please Allah ﷻ. To please Allah ﷻ, one performs acts of service to the community. The outcome is unimportant, but Allah ﷻ values the struggle along the way.

28. Love for the Last Child

There was a Sufi who used to have many children. She had a special love for her last child. This child was so nice in his character compared to the others. He had the utmost *adab*. If he made a mistake, he immediately said, "I am sorry." The Sufi was thinking about the wisdom behind it.

IN PRACTICE

Sometimes, being last can entail possessing all positive qualities. Muhammad Rasulullah ﷺ was the last of all prophets. Nevertheless, he was the most exemplary role model of good and virtuous characteristics.

29.   The Sufi and the Inviter

Sufis referred to a certain man as the Inviter. This man used to invite others to good and favorable events, but he never attended himself. Again, it was one of those days, and the Inviter told the Sufi, "There is a great lecture at the other mosque if you wish to attend." The Sufi thanked him politely for the invitation and noted with a smile that, as usual, the Inviter would not be attending the event, but rather inviting others.

In practice

Actions come before words. Expression does not require words. People have the capacity to reason and deduce meanings. Great orators have no value unless they regularly practice. Allah ﷻ values sincere endeavors, but not empty words.

30. Firing the Cleaner of the Mosque & Disappointment

An elderly man was responsible for cleaning the mosque. He was unable to speak English. However, he was close with the Sufi, and they used sign language to communicate. One day, the old man approached the Sufi in a very despondent manner and informed him that he had received a letter from administration informing him that his position as a cleaner would be terminated in 30 days. The Sufi was depressed and spoke with the administration, but their decision remained unchanged. During these 30 days, the old man visited the Sufi several times per week to inform him that his position would be terminated at the end of the month. The Sufi was overcome with sadness and thought to himself, "I wish we could only have expectations of Allah ﷻ and not of people."

In practice

As humans, we expect recognition and encouragement from others, especially if we have worked in a place for an extended period of time. Instead of appreciation, the individual is terminated with only 30 days' notice. Due to the mortal and transient nature of humans, the value of their gifts to other humans may be limited and temporary. Humans may appear to applaud or congratulate others on their accomplishments, but it is all superficial, time-based, and peripheral. If a person expects recognition only from the Infinite Allah ﷻ, then his or her accomplishments become infinite, and not time-based or temporal in comparison to human accomplishments, in the Heavenly system of infinite rewards.

31. The Farewell Visit of the Mosque Cleaner

It was the final day for the mosque's cleaner. After completing the cleaning of the mosque, he approached the Sufi. The Sufi asked for his forgiveness and then presented him with a small gift. The mosque cleaner was surprised because he had never heard the Sufi speak for many months, possibly even over a year, and they had always communicated through sign language. The Sufi smiled as the man departed, and he was saddened by the pleasant memories he shared with the mosque cleaner.

IN PRACTICE

It is essential to seek forgiveness from the people we interact with. Backbiting and violating the rights of others are grave transgressions that will require accountability before Allah ﷻ in the hereafter. Therefore, it is customary to ask for forgiveness in farewell situations, even if there is no dispute between the individuals.

32. Carrying Change

There once was a Sufi who disliked carrying loose change and cash in his pocket. He preferred having empty pockets devoid of weight. One day, a beggar approached him and requested money. He felt bad that he was unable to assist him. The following day, while he was out, a second beggar approached him and asked for money. He again felt bad about his inability to assist him. Finally, the Sufi said, "Perhaps I should carry spare change." He went out the following day. He was pleased that he had spare change in case a beggar approached him. The day passed without a beggar appearing. The Sufi was unhappy.

In practice

There are occasions, times, and obligations for each location and time. There are five prayers that must be performed within a given time period. People observe a month-long fast. They perform pilgrimage at a particular time. If these opportunities are lost, the good deed cannot be performed. Similarly, in the preceding story, although the Sufi can receive a reward from Allah ﷻ due to his intention, one must always be ready to seize opportunities at the right times in order to maintain a healthy relationship with Allah ﷻ.

33.   Troubles and Meanings

The Sufi awoke one morning with a headache. As usual, she began her day with her usual routine. She began her day with *dhikr*, meditation, and scripture recitations. As she prepared to go to work, she hoped that the day would be fast and routine, as usual, because her mind was scattered and she was unable to collect herself mentally and emotionally. With these thoughts in mind, she headed to work. She found herself in the middle of a mess at work, with everyone blaming her for something. As her mental and emotional wanderings progressed, she was unable to respond to her mental health accordingly.

In practice

It is essential to constantly recall dependence on Allah ﷻ. Occasionally, our routines undermine our dependency on Allah ﷻ. This is considered carelessness[vi]. Nonetheless, these instances of unforeseen difficulties, trials, or tests can occur at any time and in any location. Our dispositions should be to immediately seek forgiveness from Allah ﷻ for any possible error on our part, as David (PBUH) did, as recorded in the Scriptures[vii]. David (PBUH) rendered his verdict as soon as the disputing parties appeared before him to settle their dispute. However, as soon as they departed, he hurried to ask forgiveness from them due to the appearance of this unusual case as a sign from Allah ﷻ to remind him.

34.   Virus & Precautions

There was a pandemic virus. The Sufi learned of the news and immediately began taking the precautions recommended by doctors and officials. Yet, she constantly reminded herself that these were merely means and that Allah ﷻ is the Real Doer.

IN PRACTICE

It is essential to take the precautions recommended by experts. Nonetheless, it is essential to remember that if these precautions fail, then Allahﷻ's Decree[3] is the ultimate cause. During these difficult times, one should never complain about this Divine Decree, but instead maintain gratitude with the One. As Rasulullah ﷺ [52] demonstrated, it is normal for humans to grieve and feel sad. However, he never criticized the Divine Decree [52].

---

3. Qadar

35.   The Qurãn and the Water Fountains

The Sufi was traveling one day. He stopped in a village due to his thirst. The village offered numerous water fountains for travelers. As the Sufi entered the village, he observed a variety of free water fountains with distinct designs that were created for thirsty travelers. The Sufi approached a water fountain. He took a sip of water. He stated, "This is delicious." Then he thought to himself, "I want to sample the water from all of the fountains." Then, he began trying them all. He said, "*SubhanAllah!* They all possess the same exquisite and pure flavor. They must have the same source."

IN PRACTICE

The verses and chapters of the Qur'an are comparable to various water sources. If a person reads a verse, a chapter, or the entirety of the Qur'an, he or she will realize that the Author is the Same, Allah ﷻ, the Creator, regardless of whether we refer to Him as Allah, Adonai, or the One. These include the Oneness and Uniqueness of the Creator[4], accountability, justice, morality, and humans as role models.

---

4. Tawhid

36.   Nice Breezes of the Grave

It was the evening 15 days prior to Ramadan[5]. The Sufi went to the cemetery in the middle of the night to visit old friends, just as Rasulullah ﷺ did. As instructed by the Prophet, he said, [52] "Peace be upon you, my friends, my teachers, and my family from the believers! You traveled before us. We will see you soon, God willing." The Sufis then felt a pleasant spiritual breeze, as though they were hearing their response, and they were pleased that the Sufis had visited them.

In practice

The soul does not perish with the physical body when a person dies. Our souls continue to exist in another reality or dimension known as *barzahk*. In this reality, life persists. Rasulullah ﷺ knew and taught us how to interact with souls, as described in the preceding Sufi expressions. Rasulullah ﷺ used to describe the condition of the deceased in the grave in their next life. If they needed assistance, Rasulullah ﷺ taught them how to assist them [52].

---

5. Laylatul Bara'ah

37.   Effects of the Society and Humanness

As usual, the Sufi was living a life of solitude and minimal human interaction. She used to believe that she didn't care about the state of the world so long as she maintained her relationship with Allah ﷻ. One day, an pandemic spread throughout the globe. Every day, the news covering this virus. The Sufi maintained her solitude with Allah ﷻ despite being significantly perturbed. Yet, as she listened to the news in her minimal interaction with people, she thought to herself, "As a human, it is extremely difficult to avoid the effects of society, despite the fact that one can try to minimize all social proximity."

In practice

A person on the path of spirituality is not perturbed by the daily scandal on the news. Many people wake up and sleep with the news on their television, cell phone, and computer. They allow this news to manipulate their emotions, fracturing and destroying them. Yet, a person on the path has a life objective, meaning, and purpose. Daily events and scandal news have no effect on their emotions. As suggested by Rasulullah ﷺ saw [52] (#2722), the people on the path should engage with useful knowledge and information in order to achieve their lifelong goal on the path. This objective is to achieve happiness, tranquility, and peace in this life by pleasing the One who is the Source of all happiness, tranquility, and peace.

38. Angels and the Sufi

One day, the Sufi was praying in the mosque. No one was present to pray with him. Therefore, he began praying alone in the hope that angels would join him in prayer. Then, out of nowhere, a butterfly entered the room. Outside it was snowing, and it was not butterfly season. The Sufi realized this and exclaimed, "Thank God, I am not alone."

In practice

If a person does something sincerely for Allah's sake, Allah does not abandon that person. Allah can send various forms of spiritual signs to demonstrate Divine Support for this individual's sincere stance on the path. Tradition holds that angels can assume different appearances when they enter the human realm. They may take the form of humans or other beings. In the preceding story, the Sufi was convinced that Allah sent an angel in the form of a butterfly as a Divine Support.

39. Bird and the Sufi

Everyday, the Sufi would visit the mosque to pray. A bird would approach the Sufi as he left the mosque and examine his face. The bird looked like a hoopoe. As this occurred daily, the Sufi began to wonder, "Perhaps the bird wants to communicate with me." Then he began to read the Qur'anic verses describing the conversation between the hoopoe and Rasulullah ﷺ Solomon. The bird then approached the Sufi and, upon observing his face, began to chirp and speak. The Sufi wished he could comprehend what the speaker was saying.

In practice

People on the path of spirituality are able to communicate with other beings, animals, and plants. Muhammad's contemporaries witnessed stones, trees, and animals conversing with Rasulullah ﷺ on multiple occasions, according to verifiable reports. The Qur'an mentions the conversation between Solomon and the hoopoe.

40. High Expectations and Children

There was once a Sufi who had eight children. The Sufi used to be so fond of the seventh one. One day, the seventh one made a grave error in judgment. The Sufi was greatly disheartened and unable to make peace with himself over his child's grave error. Then he thought to himself, "I shouldn't sanctify anyone, not even my loved ones!"

IN PRACTICE

Humans are humans. Understanding this fact is crucial. If a person sanctifies or divinizes another person, they have committed one of the gravest errors possible. *La ilaha illa Allah* requires only a sincere attachment to Allah ﷻ. One can love someone or something, but it is essential to have a true and accurate evaluation of everything. In the preceding story, the error is the parents' false and incorrect assessment and evaluation of his child. When a child fails a parent, the parent may feel great frustration and have their hopes dashed. One should expect Allah ﷻ at all times. Allah ﷻ is the only One who never leaves a person in a state of frustration.

41.   Good Intentions and Finding Yourself in a Mess

One day, the Sufi wished to assist a friend in need. In an effort to avoid offending her friend, the Sufi was extremely cautious about how she should assist her. Her friend was the type who refused assistance from anyone. The Sufi attempted to approach her gently, but she became angry and spoke harshly. The Sufi was upset and restrained herself from responding. The Sufi thought, "You never know how a good thing can turn into a mess."

IN PRACTICE

Allah ﷻ rewards a person based on their intention, not on the outcome of what they accomplish or lose. A person with good intentions can occasionally find themselves in an unexpected circumstance. However, maintaining composure, calmness, and patience and avoiding anger is always more productive in both spiritual and worldly matters.

42. Winners and Losers

One day, a Sufi gained a lot of knowledge, piety, and respect. He started to have a lot of followers changing themselves with his teachings on the path of Allah ﷻ. The Sufi's friends and family members were also benefiting from his knowledge and teachings. They said to themselves, "We are so lucky that we have the Sufi in our lives. What a great bounty of Allah ﷻ! It is like winning a lottery!" Yet, a few of the Sufi's old friends and family members got jealous and said, "Why him? We are better than the Sufi. Why don't people follow us, but they follow him?" They became increasingly jealous of the Sufi. They lost on the path of winning.

IN PRACTICE

It is important to detect our spiritual diseases before they kill us. A person on the path of Allah ﷻ can be winning yet he or she can lose with jealousy. Satan is the primary example of this. On the other hand, an intelligent person can realize that if Allah ﷻ chooses some people to be role models such as the prophets, and saints[6], then an intelligent person can make use of this to benefit their own spiritual growth. An intelligent person benefits from the people who are the source of light and guidance as the friends of Allah ﷻ. Killing oneself with jealousy and self-destructive hatred is the worst foolishness, absurdity, and irrationality. When one reviews the life of Rasulullah ﷺ (ﷺ), everyone boosted their true spirituality with his pearl and diamond teachings. Yet, there were a few from his old friends and family members who blocked themselves due to their iron curtains built with jealousy, hatred, and arrogance in their hearts.

---

6. Awliyaullah

43.   The Ban and the Sufi

One day, the Sufi heard that the town banned people going out at night due to expected protests and vandalism. She said to herself, "People will be in fear even if nothing happens." She spent her night in regular chants, prayers, and remembrance of Allah ﷻ.

IN PRACTICE

It is important not to be trapped in current events. The maintenance of the relation with Allah ﷻ can put the person in peace and calmness even during times when many people are in the states of fear and panic. At these times, it is a responsibility to give people hope and calmness once one takes care of oneself spiritually with one's regular engagements of one's relationship with Allah ﷻ. The one who is already in the flow of fear and panic cannot help others already dragged down with daily and hourly news of magazines.

44.   The Flies in the Dream

One day, the Sufi had a dream. Some of the dirty looking flies were stuck at home on the window screen trying to leave. The Sufi helped them to leave the house. There were a bunch of them. Then, she woke up from her dream. She said, "*Alhamdulillah*, my spiritual dirty flies will leave my house."

IN PRACTICE

Sound dreams are one of the means of communication between the seen and unseen realities [53]. Dirty flies in the above dream can represent one's spiritual sicknesses such as jealousy, arrogance, and anger causing one to oppress and abuse others. A house can represent one's heart or soul, their real identity.

45. Head of the State & the Poor Man

There was a poor man in the mosque suffering from paranoia. Every day, he used to come to the Sufi in the mosque and tell him how everyone was planning against him in the mosque. One day, as usual, this poor man came to the Sufi in the mosque. He said to him, "Were you here when the head of the state came yesterday? He came here to plot against me with others in the mosque. I am a citizen of this country. They cannot kick me out." The Sufi did not say anything as usual and offered him a coffee.

In practice

Sometimes, our ungrounded fears about others overwhelm us and make us dysfunctional. If this happens constantly, then it can become an illness referred to as persecution complex or paranoia which can lead to psychosis. Yet, it is important to diagnose it in its early stages before it becomes an illness. On the spiritual path, having a good spiritual teacher, a good collective meditation group, a good friend, and daily regular personal spiritual practices as *awrad* can be some of the means to detect and remove the seeds of these diseases before they grow further. Reliance on Allah ﷻ constantly with *La ilaha illa Allah*, removing and discharging oneself from all fears and anxieties with this chant, and regular daily prayers can be some of the practical remedies that can prevent building plaque on the heart and mind causing emotional and mental disorders.

46.   Religious Leaders, Institution, and Balance

One day, the Sufi attended a gathering. One of the priests of the mosque was proud to explain how one day a guy came to the mosque to pray but he did not want to follow the guidelines of the mosque. This person started arguing with the priest. The priest was firm about the rules. The guy left and did not come back again. Although the priest seemed to be following the guidelines of his institution, his confident way of narrating this incident to others made the Sufi uncomfortable.

In practice

One should be always scared of breaking anyone's heart even though he or she may be right at the end of the argument. This attitude is so critical and can become deadly especially in the interactions with people coming to religious institutions and communicating with the representatives of the religion. In the above story, the Sufi was disturbed due to the self-assured attitude of the priest. The Sufi expected a sorrowful and empathetic feeling (you might consider using the word compassionate) for the guy from the priest although he needed to implement institutional guidelines. One can find this often in the life of Rasulullah ﷺ ﷺ. When a person made reparations for his evil act, some people cursed the person. Upon hearing this, Rasulullah ﷺ ﷺ got very upset and said, "This person did such a repentance in front of Allah ﷻ that can be sufficient for all the city in Medina, [53]." Humility requires having empathy for others.

47. Coldness in Attitude and Balance

One day, the Sufi happened to meet one of his friends that he had not seen for a long time. As soon as the Sufi realized that it was him, he ran to his old friend and said, "How are you? I hope everything is good. I didn't see you for a long time." His friend did not seem to be warm and welcoming. He replied, "Fine, thank you." The Sufi felt sad and said to himself, "Did I do anything wrong? I didn't see him for a long time. Therefore, I was excited. Why his attitude is so cold?"

IN PRACTICE

It is important to greet the person at least in the same manner as the greeter. The better is to greet the other with even more expressions of peace and even more excitement. This way is the way of Rasulullah ﷺ ﷺ [54]. Sometimes, a person's spiritual state can overcome the person. This can make the person not adapt to their surroundings easily. Yet, the person is expected to be aware of the realities and do their best effort not to offend people and disappoint people's expectations.

48.   The Sufi and the Ant

One day, the Sufi was studying in the mosque. There was an ant walking on the carpet. The Sufi said, "Let me help her. It looks like she has lost her way." He took a paper towel to hold the ant. He was trying to hold the ant but she did not want to come. After a little struggle, the ant seemed to lose her energy. The Sufi screamed, "Please don't die! That wasn't my intention." The Sufi immediately rushed to bring some water and date pieces to give to the ant so that the ant could survive. The Sufi was crying and praying to Allah ﷻ for the ant's life. After some time, the ant seemed to start walking again. The Sufi said, "*Alhamdulillah!*"

IN PRACTICE

Everything that has a life is a reminder of the One, al-Hayy, the Source of Life, Allah ﷻ. Everything makes *dhikr*, remembrance of Allah ﷻ. Therefore, everything is a real friend except some humans in loss who are not in remembrance of Allah ﷻ. Yet, one should even treat them as potential friends with their possible guidance by Allah ﷻ.

49. The Sufi and "My Best Friend the Tree"

There was a Sufi who used to love all of the creation as connected to the Source of the Life, al-Hayy. One day, the people were arguing if they should cut the tree down adjacent to the mosque. They said, "We need to cut it down because its roots can damage the structure of the building." The Sufi opposed the idea and said, "We should not kill a tree that is alive." After a while, the discussion was over. Majority seemed to think that they should cut the tree down. After a few weeks, it was a sunny nice day. The Sufi came to the mosque and while he was walking to the entrance, he fainted at the door. After a while people rushed to the Sufi. The Sufi woke up. He was crying about the tree that was cut. The Sufi said, "My best friend is dead."

IN PRACTICE

All the living beings remember and make the *dhikr* of Allah. Everything is a friend that connects the person with them. The Sufi was devastated in the above story by witnessing the death of one of his best friends, the tree.

50.   Silly Things Turn Into Big Problems

One day, the Sufi was thinking about how simple and silly things can cause big problems if they are not handled gently and with wisdom and patience. He said to himself, "Anything at work, at mosque/temple, at home and even with friends. Wow! SubhanAllah! Very challenging, yet it looks like a piece of cake! Maybe, it should be called a "piece-of-cake looking minefield!""

IN PRACTICE

The notion of *fitnah* can be defined as chaos in societies, in families, and even in any type of relationship. The starting point of *fitnah* can be something silly and it can grow if it is not handled carefully and taken care of with wisdom and patience. Some may refer to this as early stage cancer cells as compared to the ones in the later stages that can kill people as they kill relationships. They can cause social, family, kinship and friendship chaos, aggression, violence, animosity, and disconnected relationships or diasporas at group or community levels. Therefore, the person should not take anything easy or as a "piece of cake" in life but remain always in the state of uncertainty; yet at the same time, stay in the state of tranquility by praying to Allah ﷻ for protection and striving to have a very strong relationship with Allah ﷻ regularly.

Discussion Questions

- ► What do you do in your life to address small problems before they grow into big problems? At work? At school? At home? In relationships?
- ► How do you manage your stress as you strive to balance the many aspects of your life?
- ► Do you notice a connection between how much care you are putting into your spiritual life and how well you are able to manage your daily stresses?

51.   Balance in Sharing What You Know

There was a Sufi who used to think about the personalities who like to share and go over their limits and the ones who don't care to share about what they know. Then, he said to himself, "What is the ideal model?" Then, he said, "The balance."

IN PRACTICE

There is a balance in sharing religious knowledge. The person does not try to proselytize to people. The Qur'an mentions that "there is no compulsion in religion." In other verses, the Qur'an mentions that if Allah ﷻ wanted, everyone on the earth would believe in Allah ﷻ. At the same time, if a person is benefitting from a spiritual knowledge, the person welcomes the people who want to learn in order to address their own problems. In classical Sufi writings, this is expressed as a caravan and everyone is welcome to join of their own choice.

52.   Miracles, Randomness & Determinism

The Sufi was enjoying her new life. She was saying constantly, "*Alhamdulillah*" for the miracles in her daily life. She was trying to increase her knowledge about Allah ﷻ constantly but trying to maintain humility with weakness by praying to Allah ﷻ regularly so that she did not become lost on the spiritual path. Then, she thought about her old life much with misery, doubt, arrogance, hardship, and chaos. Everything seemed to be random in those years of darkness. As she was comparing her past and present, she said to herself, "*SubhanAllah!*, This is the difference: As the person detaches oneself from Allah ﷻ with doubt, ingratitude, and arrogance, then Allah ﷻ leaves this person in that state with darkness, and depressive states of randomness and chaos. But, when the person realizes his or her real self with weakness, need, purpose, and connecting to the One, Allah ﷻ with *iman*, belief and appreciation, then Allah ﷻ opens all the doors of light, tranquility, easiness and even constant daily miracles to approve this correct and true disposition.

In practice

As the person sets off on the journey with humility in one's relationship with Allah ﷻ, then Allah ﷻ opens all the doors of signs. One may call this miracles. Then, the person starts living a wonder-filled and a heaven-like life in this world before she or he dies and goes to the heaven in the afterlife.

53. Levels and Tastes: Columbian Roast vs Breakfast Blend Coffee

The Sufi always used to drink breakfast blend coffee. She did not like other blends. One day, she realized that she had bought the wrong blend of coffee-the Columbian roast. She did not have time to go return it to the store. So she made a pot of coffee using the Columbian Roast. After the first sip, she said to herself, "*Alhamdulillah*, I didn't know I liked the Columbian roast as well!"

IN PRACTICE

As the person changes physically over the time, the person also changes spiritually. A thorough engagement with one spiritual state can be painful; but at another time, it can have a good taste and bring pleasure. Tasting differentiation is a skill. Different brews of coffee taste differently to different people at different times. For one, external appearances may look like suffering but internally there is joy.

Discussion Questions

- ▶ Describe a situation when you and someone else had different emotional reactions to the same event. What factors do you think played a role in how each of you experienced that event internally?
- ▶ Is there any significant experience in your life that you had a very different response to and perspective about when going through a second time? How about a third time?
- ▶ Have you been surprised by your own responses to some of life's surprises? What do you make of them?

54. Learning for a Purpose

One day, the Sufi was thinking about why people learn. She said to herself, "There are a lot of people who learn but they don't benefit themselves. Is this knowledge still useful? Is learning just any knowledge useful?"

In practice

Knowledge can be distracting if there is no purpose and no application. Rasulullah ﷺ teaches and Allah ﷻ asks us to learn useful and beneficial knowledge. In other words, knowledge can be distracting from one's relationship with Allah ﷻ if there is no purpose to it, if there is no benefit, and ultimately, if there is no application of the acquired knowledge by the person.

Discussion Questions

- ► What kind of knowledge is useful to you in your life?
- ► What knowledge do you personally find to be without purpose in your life?

55. Child and the Parents

One day, the Sufi visited a family and witnessed an interaction between the child and parents. The child said to the parents, "You did not do anything for me. I don't care about you." The mom said, "Oh my son! Do you remember the days that I used to change your diapers, breastfeed you, and take you to your school? Do you remember the days that your dad used to take care of you, teach you, and get what you needed?" The child said, "I don't care. I don't want to know you in my life." The Sufi did not like the environment and said to herself, "What an ungrateful child! This is exactly the same and the worst case- when the person does not recognize Allah ﷻ and is ungrateful to their Creator."

IN PRACTICE

It is required to respect, acknowledge, and appreciate one's parents regardless of if they are good or bad. Even in disputes of religion, Allah ﷻ orders their kind treatment in the Qurān [55]. The relationship of the person with their parents can be a measuring stick for the people to judge their relationship with the Creator. The Creator, Allah ﷻ, has more rights on a person than the parents. Yet, there are a lot of people who tend to deny these rights.

56. Alien, the Sufi and Cutting Nails

There was an alien who came from another planet. Allah ﷻ gave the alien different abilities not too similar to humans. For example, the alien could be cut into pieces and unlike humans, would not feel any pain, and then could be put back together into its full body again. The alien witnessed the humans suffering if something happened to their bodies. One day, the alien saw the Sufi on a Friday cutting his nails. The alien got shocked and said to the Sufi, "Are you an alien like me! I see that if humans cut any part of the body, they are in so much pain and screaming! Yet you are cutting your nails and seem to still be happy and not in any pain!"

In practice

Our bodies are just bodies. It does not have much value compared to the value of soul. In other words, it has a value and deserves respect because Allah ﷻ created it. Yet, the real purpose is not the bodily endeavors. If Allah ﷻ wants, humans can be equipped with different physical frames called bodies similar to the alien's body in the above story. Perhaps, the body parts such as nails or hair are given to humans without any sensory awareness by Allah ﷻ to remind us of this reality although all of the other body parts are surrounded by the nervous system and are capable of receiving pain.

Discussion Questions

- Do you ever have a sense that you are more than your body?
- Do you ever feel stuck in your body?
- Do you find that you take balanced care of your body and soul, or better care of one or the other?
- What can you do to take better care of your soul?
- How can you use your body to take better care of your soul?

57. Mission and Over

One day, the Sufi was thinking about her mission in the world. She was deeply thinking about the following questions: "Does death mean that the mission is over?" "If so, what is my mission?" "Can I decide when my mission is over?" or "Without my choice, is the mission over?"

In practice

The mission in the world is to please Allah ﷻ by working on oneself, by training one's ego with worship, gratitude, and joy. At the same time the mission is to serve humanity in order to please Allah ﷻ. Some people can dedicate their entire lives and death comes indicating that the mission is over. They don't choose the end of the mission. Some elect people, like Rasulullah ﷺ Muhammad, are asked by Allah ﷻ through angels, if they want to stay in the world longer for the mission or be with the Beloved, Allah ﷻ [54].

58. Healthy Fear

One day, the Sufi was driving home on a Friday night passing a few bars where some people were drinking. On the street, there was a big billboard showing a crying parent who lost their children due to a drunk driver. Another billboard next to it was showing scary police and the imprisonment of a drunk driver with the huge fines for drunk drivers. The Sufi got scared and felt disturbed. After collecting himself from the scenes of drinking people in the bar and the billboard signs, he said to himself, "Fear has a place and it is not always evil."

In practice

Sometimes, we go through different emotional cycles during the day. In some emotional states, we may not care about hurting others. At these times, as mentioned in the above story, if the person has the fear of consequences of his or her goofy actions, then he or she may stop doing it. Similarly, on the spiritual path, sometimes, the person can feel so pumped up with joy, self-satisfaction and certainty. If the person does not have the fear of accountability in front of Allah ﷻ, then the person can have vanity and arrogance while being called a "religious person." Fear has different levels. Some people fear and stop their own evil in order to not be punished in Hell because they want to be in Heaven. This can be a good starting point. Yet, this can be a beginner's level. Some people have fear and stop their own evil in order not to displease Allah ﷻ because they love and appreciate Allah ﷻ so much. This can be the level of the elect on the spiritual path.

59. Heart & Mind

One day, the Sufi was enjoying her prayers and fasting so much. She did not want to continue much learning and using her mind. Yet, she felt guilty about it. Another day, she was enjoying learning so much she did not continue her prayers and fasting other than the required ones. Yet, she felt guilty about it. She said to herself, "I know the key is balance as Rasulullah ﷺ SAW suggested."

IN PRACTICE

Rasulullah ﷺ teaches us the balance between heart and mind. Rasulullah ﷺ was always in deep meditation, prayers and worship, yet Rasulullah ﷺ smiled, ate, and socialized nicely and kindly with his family members and people. Even during the journey of ascension[viii], Rasulullah ﷺ was offered to be in Heaven where one's emotions and feelings can overpower the person. Yet, Rasulullah ﷺ SAW used the faculties of both his mind and heart to come back to earth in order to fulfill and complete his mission. The balance is very difficult. Yet, it is the goal.

Discussion Questions

- How could I bring more balance into my life right now? Which 2 areas are being neglected and which 2 areas are taking most of my energy?
- Which relationships in my life need more attention right now?
- Does my relationship with Allah ﷻ need more attention?

60. Our Role Model

One day, the Sufi was thinking about our role models. She was thinking about the life of Rasulullah ﷺ Muhammad and how he lived a life without breaking hearts. Everyone loved him. He was truthful. Then, the Sufi said, "*Alhamdulillah*, we are so lucky to have such role models so that we can realize that humans do achieve to become real humans although we have a lot of challenges and difficulties.

In practice

It is important to have teachers who show and apply the teachings in their lives as role models. Rasulullah ﷺ Muhammad embodied all the teachings in his own life. Therefore, people practiced his teachings not due to experiencing a formal lecture format but by observing him and impersonating him as their role model.

Discussion Questions

- ► What has been the value in your life of living role models?
- ► Have you been inspired by legends of role models passed down? What inspired you?
- ► What important teachings have you absorbed in your life that you did not learn in a classroom?
- ► What important teachings do you strive to embody, allowing people to witness that there are people like you out there?

61.   The Punishment of the Tree and the Sufi

There was a Sufi who used to drive a cool sports car. One day, he went to the mosque and parked his car under a tree. While he was closing the windows, the leaves of the tree were stuck in the windows. The Sufi saw this and said to himself, "When I come back I can open the windows to take the leaves out." After a few hours, the Sufi came to his car. As soon as he drove away, he heard a light scream. He looked around and said, "Oh my Allah ﷻ! I forgot the branches stuck in my windows. I hope the tree was not upset with me." As the Sufi was driving the car, the Sufi saw light raindrops on his car's windshield. He turned on the wipers. The wipers seemed to not wipe away this rain. The Sufi said, "I don't understand. This is a new car. The wipers should be new, too." The Sufi could not see well and barely made it home. When he got out of the car, he touched the windshield and there was a sticky substance thickly smothering the car. The Sufi said, "The punishment of the tree!"

In practice

Everything remembers Allah ﷻ and chants in its own language except some humans and jinn. Hurting them for no reason can require compensation. There are rulings in practice not to cut tree branches. If people do it there can be some measures taken against the person. In the above story, the tree released some type of sticky substance on the Sufi's car due to its branch being cut unjustly.

62. Missing the Prayer & Marriage Problems

One day, the Sufi had an argument with her husband. She was upset with him and did not want to talk to him. He was also too proud to use wisdom. He said to himself, "If she doesn't want to talk, I am also not going to talk." They slept as usual together in the same bed. Both fell asleep and missed the morning (fajr) prayer. Both woke up very upset because of missing the prayer. The Sufi said to herself, "Possibly, this may be a sign of the displeasure of Allah ﷻ about useless and purposeless argumentation between the couple leading to broken hearts.

IN PRACTICE

The one who has the upper hand is the one who can control his or her lowly selfish desires of anger, pride, and arrogance in human and especially marital relationships. Our egos naturally incline to show these signs if they are not trained or disciplined. One of the important displeasures of Allah ﷻ is about the disputes and arguments between couples. In practice, divorce is permissible but one of the disliked options of Allah ﷻ. The person is expected not to act childishly, especially in marital affairs. If one is acting in these manners, then the other should strive even harder to uphold the principles of marriage loved by Allah ﷻ. In gender identities of marriage, man is expected to establish peace in the family moreso than the woman. If the wife gets angry, the husband is expected to be on the calm side, to smile, and to let it go. This is the underlying notion in the teachings of the Qur'an in different verses[7]. If one analyzes the relationship of Rasulullah ﷺ with women, it is in his extra gentle, calm, and soft manners [50].

Discussion Questions

- ▶ What could I say to my spouse when we are in conflict that might disarm the emotional state we have co-created and give us a chance to start anew?
- ▶ What prevents me from seeking peace when I know I want peace?
- ▶ How can I use my relationship with Allah ﷻ to guide my conflict

---

7. Such as [4:34]

resolution practices?

63.   Vanilla Ice Cream and the Sufi

There was a Sufi from Turkey who had a hard time pronouncing the word vanilla and yet, he loved vanilla ice cream. In Turkish, there are no letters differentiating the sounds between w and v. Again, one day, the Sufi went to a drive-thru to buy ice cream for his kids and himself. He said, "Can I please get three baby cone vanilla ice creams?" The cashier on the speaker at the drive-thru said, "Sir, what did you want, could you repeat it again?" The Sufi repeated himself, but again, the cashier didn't understand. After a few times of going back and forth, the cashier, said, "Sir, sorry, I think we have some problem at our speaker system. Sorry for the inconvenience. If you could kindly pull up to the window, we can take your order there."

IN PRACTICE

It is always preferred to assume good for others. Although the person may know others' mistakes and spiritual diseases, it is a spiritual level and maturity to gently address these issues without directly pointing or blaming the person. In the above story, the cashier gently addressed the problem without making the Sufi feel bad.

Discussion Questions

- ▶ Give an example of how you might politely address someone's misbehavior without embarrassing the person.
- ▶ Give an example of how someone has politely addressed your misbehavior without embarrassing you.
- ▶ What is the benefit of assuming the good for others? How does that benefit others and how does it benefit you?

64.   Computer Cord

One day, the Sufi was working on her computer. There was a bunch of books next to the computer. The computer was plugged in to the outlet for charging. There were books on the cord, covering it, and the Sufi had forgotten about them. After a few hours of studying, the Sufi wanted to take a break and wanted to unplug her computer. Then, she started pulling the cord. She applied force to pull the cord but for some reason the cord seemed to be stuck somewhere. Then, she realized the problem. She gently held the piles of the books to swiftly retract the cord. She did it and said, "*Alhamdulillah*, if I pulled the cord harshly, all the books would have fallen on the floor and made a big mess."

IN PRACTICE

It is important to use gentleness and wisdom when solving difficulties. Sometimes, we tend to apply more force with harshness to solve problems in human relations. Yet, this can aggravate the issue more, make a big mess, and even break relationships. The Sufi realized a similar trend in our physical interactions with objects.

65. Loyalty to the Old Shoes

The Sufi had old shoes. He was still using them and liked them very much. His wife was getting angry with the Sufi about not throwing these old shoes in the garbage. One day, the Sufi was wearing other shoes and he was not home. His wife used this opportunity to throw away his old shoes. When the Sufi came home he couldn't find his shoes and asked his wife about it and she said, "I put them in a bag outside to be thrown in the garage. They will be thrown away." The Sufi smiled and did not say anything. He found the bag and retrieved his shoes and started wearing them again. His wife got angry but didn't say anything to the Sufi. After a few months, the Sufi was not home. His wife was cleaning the garage and again saw the Sufi's old shoes. She took then and put them at the bottom of the garbage can. After a while, the Sufi came and wanted to wear his shoes. He asked his wife about his shoes, she said, "They are in the garbage." The Sufi went to the garbage and started searching for his shoes. It was so difficult with the bad smell for the Sufi because Sufis are repelled by bad smells. With all his effort, he couldn't find his shoes. He was upset and it was garbage day.

IN PRACTICE

The loyalty to our old friends, teachers, and especially to our parents are critical. One should not dump old, good relationships with others as one changes in life. Rasulullah ﷺ also had relationship and appreciation with objects such as a hair brush that he was using. In the above story, the Sufi wanted to carry this perspective of loyalty for his old shoes.

Discussion Questions

- ▶ Who are you loyal to and who is loyal to you? What is important about the loyalty in these relationships?
- ▶ Do you have any things or activities in your life that you are loyal to as well? Why?
- ▶ What is it about your loyalty that makes it an important part of your life?

66.   The Mirrors & the Kids

One day, the Sufi was thinking about which of her kids she is most similar to in character. She had three children. After a while of thinking hard, she said, "My childhood is similar to the youngest one. My present character is similar to the middle one. Perhaps, my old age character will be similar to the oldest one."

In practice

It is important to realize that Allah ﷻ is fair and just. Allah ﷻ sends us people, events, or things to see our own selves. Yet, we don't seem to take lessons from them but rather see them as external events, or things related with others. One of the biggest mirrors among them is a person's own children.

Discussion Questions

- ► What have your children taught you about yourself?
- ► Who else in your life acts as a mirror for you?

67. Pain in the Eye & the Prayer

One day, the Sufi had a pain in his eye. He was thinking about what he should do. Then, he remembered the *dua,* the prayer of Rasulullah ﷺ about pains of the eye. He put his hand over his eye and read the *dua* as suggested by the Prophet. The pain was immediately gone.

IN PRACTICE

It is important to follow all the teachings of the Prophet. If one applies these simple-looking but very effective teachings then one can avoid a lot different kinds of pain in life easily and quickly. In the above story, the Sufi applied the Prophetic Teachings immediately instead of rushing to take a medicine from the pharmacy or calling a doctor.

Discussion Questions

- ► Do you ever use holistic medicines for common ailments?

68. Train Ride Nowhere

One day, the Sufi was riding on the train in Boston. It was rush hour in the morning. The Sufi was calmly sitting on the train, disconnecting from her surroundings and making her *dhikr*. She then for a second put her head up and realized everyone was looking at their cellphones and they were also disconnected from their surroundings. Then, the Sufi smiled and said to herself, "Orthodox and post-modern Sufi-looking people."

IN PRACTICE

Disconnection from one's physical medium is a virtue as long as this is disconnection takes the person to a better spiritual state. If the disconnection aggravates the person's focus with more distraction, one should reconsider the effects of this disconnection. In the above story, cell phones can be tools for the representations of the modern Sufi-looking engagements.

Discussion Questions

- ▶ What are some ways the cell phone can be used to promote a better spiritual state?
- ▶ What are some other activities that could be done on a train ride to promote a better spiritual state?

69. Honoring the Guest

There were two Sufis, one liked having guests and the other did not as much. The one who liked the guests honored his guests and treated them so nicely. Then, the guests and the Sufi became lifelong friends in this world and even in the afterlife. The other Sufi did not honor his guests much. Although he knew and understood its importance, he did not honor his guests much for some reason. Then, the guests felt broken-hearted and not treated well. Later in life, they became evil-seeming enemies.

IN PRACTICE

Every trial, test, and difficulty can be a guest. If the person honors them by saying *Alhamdullilah*, and stays grateful and appreciative to Allah ﷻ, then these evil-seeming incidents can become friends, as a means of salvation in this world and in the afterlife. However, if the person complains and severs relationship with Allah ﷻ, then the person can lose happiness both in this world and in the afterlife.

70. The Mosque Administrators

One day, the Sufi was traveling. He visited a mosque during his travels. He said to himself, "Let me go to the early morning prayer and stay there for a few hours to do my *wird*." After the morning prayer was over the administrators of the mosque came to the Sufi and said that they needed to close the mosque.

In practice

It is important to help travelers and use the prayer places for the purpose suggested by the Prophet. Unfortunately, there are a lot of people who seem to follow the policies of institutions but not follow genuinely and mercifully the pearl and diamond teachings of the Prophet.

71. Bee Confident

There was a confident Sufi who used to give advice about bees. He used to say, "As long as you don't bother the bees they don't sting you." One day, he went out in the backyard with his wife to sit in the gazebo. There was a bee around his wife. His wife got very nervous and agitated. The Sufi said, "As long as you don't bother the bees they don't sting you." He smiled confidently and the bee left. One day, the Sufi was walking under a tree and he heard a buzzing sound around his neck. He got nervous and started thinking, "If this bee stung me on my neck, I could be hospitalized." Then, he panicked and put his hand on his neck, and immediately felt the pain. The confident Sufi was stung by a bee. He smiled bitterly to himself, changed slightly his usual motto and said, "As long as you don't fret and panic when the bees are around, *then* they don't sting you."

In practice

In spiritual journeys, and life endeavors, sometimes rush or panic modes can cause more damage than expected benefits due to rushing or panicking. Especially, the term *fitnah* can be translated as the times of panic when there is uncertainty in engagements. Rasulullah ﷺ suggests to be passive and not active in those times even though there can be an expected benefit [52]. In the Qur'an, it is mentioned that the long-term harms of a *fitnah* can be more damaging than short-term explicit harms [2:191].

72. Lost Data on the Computer

One day, the Sufi was working on her computer. The computer shut down with an error. The Sufi started thinking the message behind it was that nothing happens randomly.

IN PRACTICE

It is important to personalize each incident in one's life. There are different signs that are sent to us constantly by Allah ﷻ. Yet, if we seem to not care, then the magnitude of these signs can change until one understands and gets the message. Yet, there are ones who die without deciphering these meanings and applying them in their lives. They are shown the realities of everything without any full interpretation until immediately after death but this can be too late.

Discussion Questions

- ➤ What are you grateful to have already learned now while you are still living?

73. Monitoring the Heart

There was a Sufi who used to teach the elite of society. The Sufi was trying to control her heart within the position and among the prestigious identities of her students. As she was trying to monitor her heart for any type of disease, she felt some type of anxiety, fear, and uneasiness before and after teaching her students. She understood and detected this sickness and said to herself, "The viruses are entering my heart. That is the reason why I feel uneasy and fearful. I need to practice more detachment."

IN PRACTICE

The person always makes one's intention to please Allah. If this intention is slightly affected by other means, then the person can be immediately diseased. The initial symptoms of this disease can be fear, anxiousness, and uneasiness. One should constantly go back to the embodiment of detachment phrases such as *La ilaha illa Allah* and physical prayers accompanied with tears to clean the filth. If this cleaning is not done regularly and immediately, the disease can spread in all spiritual faculties. Therefore, there is no guarantee of one's pure and full relationship with Allah until one dies. The person should be in a constant state of spiritual alertness and monitoring of their heart.

74.   Password & Keeping Secrets

There was a small girl who used to tell others about her family life incidents related to her parents and siblings. The Sufi mother used to advise her that there are things that should remain only within the family and that others do not need to and should not know. One day, this girl's cousin came to see her. They used to be best friends. While the two girl-cousins were playing together next to the Sufi outside, the wind closed the door of the house. The guest-cousin needed to go inside the house to get a drink of water and asked her cousin, "Can you please tell me the passcode so that I can go inside?" The girl went to her mom and said in a whispering voice, "Should I tell her?" The mom smiled and said, "This is not a secret. She is your cousin. She can go inside the house."

IN PRACTICE

There are many secrets that one should keep with Allah. Exposing them can make the person lose that intimate, trust-based relationship. Similarly, in a family, among husband, wife, and children there can be some secrets. Exposing them to others can make the people lose the close relationships and break the trust among them. Secrets with Allah and others are all trusts that one should not betray.

75. Positions, Disgust & Need

One day, the Sufi was thinking about why people take positions and titles for themselves in life. It is all responsibility, accountability, and yet at the same time, these things carry within them self-deceptions coming from arrogance, and desire for fame and recognition. Then, the Sufi was disgusted and said, "*Alhamdulillah*, I just want to be a normal, simple man for people but a man of value *inshAllah* known only by Allah ﷻ."

IN PRACTICE

One of the diseases is the desire for recognition and applause by people. The person can be in certain positions to fulfill a need. Yet, it is very important to always control one's heart and replace himself or herself with people of more worthiness.

76.   Scratching the Body

One day, the Sufi was doing her meditation. As she was enjoying the *dhikr*, the tip of her middle toe felt tingly and the Sufi looked at her toe and touched it and started scratching it. While she was touching her toe, she was looking at it and reflecting on the shape of the toe, and its purpose on the body. After a few minutes she said to herself, "Wow, now I understand why we need to scratch different parts of our body. It is to realize what we have been given by Allah ﷻ and appreciate it."

In practice

It is important not to take things for granted. Most of the time we have a lot but we don't realize and appreciate it. We keep our heedlessness or 'I don't care' attitude with other fellows and especially with Allah ﷻ. Sometimes simple things like scratching the body as in the above story can be sufficient for the ones who are trying to practice appreciation and awareness of Allah ﷻ and other fellows. Sometimes, big things such as evil-seeming incidents of losses, trials, and tragedies are not sufficient to wake up the person from their sleep of heedlessness.

Discussion Questions

- ▶ Describe an experience you have had similar to the story which helped you realize how important every small part is to the whole being.
- ▶ Have you ever lost something and felt a greater sense of appreciation for the thing when it was returned to you? What was that like? Did you turn to Allah ﷻ for help during that time?

77. Prescriptions for the Heart

There was a Sufi who used to have a hard time understanding people and treating them accordingly. It took him one year to understand a person. Another person, it took two years for the Sufi to understand. There are ones whom the Sufi still does not understand. The Sufi said to himself, "Once you understand them, then you can treat them accordingly."

In practice

Sometimes, we don't understand our differences related to gender, age, and culture. We insist on our stance without contextualizing the differences and normalizing them. Once the person normalizes the seeming differences, then the empathy can develop. Genuine empathy can lead to genuine communication, helping others, and learning from others. Rasulullah ﷺ (PBUH) always used to give different answers to the same question for different people as the person who was the ultimate embodiment of empathy, kindness, and gentleness.

78.   Signs & the Earthquake

It was early Thursday morning and the Sufi was reading her daily Qur'an in the mosque. She kept falling asleep while reading a page where there were some punishments mentioned about the ungrateful ones. The Sufi woke up and tried to read the same page again. She again fell asleep while reading the same page. This happened a few times. There was a heavy rain with darkness outside. The Sufi woke up one more time, glanced outside the window and said to herself, "Something is going on. May Allah SWT protect us and all of us." Shortly thereafter, the Sufi got a text message from her husband about news of a major earthquake in the city where her parents live.

In practice

Everything is a sign from Allah ﷻ in life. Allah ﷻ does not give life without any purpose and goal. Each second or minute of a person's life has a meaning and a purpose. No occurrence in life is by chance or by luck. Everything has a meaning if the person understands. If the person does not understand, anything big or small does not make any difference for this person due to that person's heedlessness or 'I don't care' attitude.

79.   The Signs

One day, the Sufi visited her friend around noon. Her friend asked the Sufi, "What is *ajal*?" The Sufi said, "It is the end time of a person, or expiration of their life." As the Sufi was leaving her friend's house, she was thinking to herself, "Why did she ask me that word out of nowhere? Was this a sign?" Later in the afternoon as the Sufi was working on her computer, she turned on her cell phone. She saw a text from an old friend that she had not spoken to for a long time. The text was about one of her close friends who had passed away in an accident. Her friend that she had visited in the morning and the one who had died did not know each other. The Sufi said to herself, "*Inna lillahi wa inna ilayhi Rajiun*, and now, I got the sign- *ajal*."

IN PRACTICE

Everything has a purpose. Allah ☝ sends different signs with different purposes. Sometimes, it is to comfort the person, sometimes to warn the person or to prepare the person for upcoming incidents and engagements. The expression "Inna lillahi wa inna ilayhi Rajiun" can translate as "We indeed belong to Allah ☝; we indeed will go back to Allah ☝."

80.   See No Evil

The Sufi was watching a cartoon with her kids on a Saturday night. They were eating popcorn, ice cream, and melted nacho cheese with crackers. Everyone seemed to enjoy watching. Yet, the Sufi was critically thinking about the representations in the cartoon. She said to herself, "What if my kids see similar looking people on the street? They will all be scared. Representations!"

IN PRACTICE

Our memories are built through our minds and hearts and they are not garbage. We cannot watch things and then not think about their consequences. Every piece of spiritual garbage inhaled, seen, heard, or experienced will affect our lifelong memories in this life and in the afterlife. Looking, seeing, and watching are all *ni'mah*, bounty from Allah ﷻ. If this bounty is not used with other ones in their proper prescribed ways then they will be witnessing against us as mentioned in the Qur'an [41:21], [56].

Discussion Questions

- ► In what ways has your media consumption negatively informed your views of stereotypes?
- ► Do you avoid any types of media as part of your spiritual lifestyle?
- ► How might you use media to enhance your relationship with Allah ﷻ?

81. Our Allah ﷻ First

One day, the Sufi attended an interfaith gathering. The Sufi said our Allah ﷻ is the Same, One, and Unique Creator whether we say Allah ﷻ, Elohim, or Allah. All the beautiful and perfect names belong to Allah ﷻ. There were some who wanted to emphasize that their Allah ﷻ was different. The Sufi said to herself, "I don't know why we are jealous of sharing our One and Unique Creator and getting into these lowly identity issues and problems."

IN PRACTICE

First, it is important to find common ground and shared values and beliefs before one discusses the differences. Being so excited about talking about differences can indicate some spiritual diseases such as jealousy and arrogance. This can be very dangerous in the discourses of religious topics and discussions both in this world and in the afterlife.

82.   Talking About or to Allah ﷻ?

One day, the Sufi attended a spiritual retreat. The retreat was about relationships with Allah ﷻ. One of the speakers said, "I think we have talked sufficiently about Allah ﷻ. Now, let's talk to Allah ﷻ through prayer." The Sufi said to herself, "Wow! SubhanAllah, this is an interesting statement." Then, she started thinking about this statement.

IN PRACTICE

It is interesting to realize that sometimes a person or especially a genuine teacher makes a statement and it really makes a mark on the person's heart and mind. This one simple-looking statement can lead to a lot of spiritual openings for the person. Most of the time, it is not due to the skills of an eloquent speaker but the power or heaviness of the words, phrases, or statements coming from the heart of the person and penetrating the hearts of others. As one looks at the life of Rasulullah ﷺ Muhammad, he said few words in his conversations [57]. Yet, it was sufficient to transform individuals and societies. The unfortunate ignorant and naive witnessed this transformation but they did not rationalize the power of this change and called Rasulullah ﷺ or genuine teachers magicians [38:4], [56].

83.   Spiritual Activist

One day, the Sufi attended a lecture. The lecturer said, "Spiritual activism is our solution to face the conflicts, problems, and evils in life and in the world. We should all be spiritual activists." The Sufi was thinking about the implications of this phrase.

In practice

Spiritual activism can indicate the spiritual power of the person through prayers, recitation of the scripture and *dhikrs* by connecting via different means to Allah ﷻ. If a person is spiritually active, then this can lead to genuine, sincere and effective individuals as social activists. There are a lot of social activists who die in their engagements due to not being fed correctly and regularly through the food of spiritual activism.

Discussion Questions

- ▸ How can a person activate spiritually in their relationship with Allah ﷻ?
- ▸ How can a person improve their relationship with Allah ﷻ through social activism?

84.   Just a Face in the Crowd

The Sufi attended a deep and powerful retreat. Some were asking from Allah SWT for some spiritual openings. The Sufi was cautious and said to herself and prayed, "Oh Allah, I want to be a normal and ordinary human as long as You are pleased with me. I don't want any spiritual openings that may come with tests and trials."

IN PRACTICE

Anything given can come with tests and trials. The purpose of tests and trials is to ensure that the person still maintains a sincere, grateful, and appreciative relationship with Allah ﷻ. There are a lot of individuals in practice who do not want extraordinary spiritual powers but only want to be normal, simple, unknown and ordinary human beings with whom Allah ﷻ is pleased. In reality, this disposition can boost the person vertically in their relation with Allah ﷻ. Rasulullah ﷺ Muhammad was the embodiment of this normality. When Rasulullah ﷺ was given the choice of being a king prophet or a normal human like others, Rasulullah ﷺ wanted to be the second option. This choice delivered him the highest attainment in spiritual journeys of Allah ﷻ.

Discussion Questions

- ▸ What are some of the advantages of remaining unknown while you achieve your spiritual and worldly goals?
- ▸ How can these advantages help you ultimately thrive spiritually and in the world?
- ▸ What are some of the emotional and intellectual obstacles the ego-driven *nafs* presents that you must struggle to overcome even though you accept how valuable it is to remain humble and ordinary?

85. Being Loaded

One day, the Sufi was waiting for her bus at the bus station. Someone was watching a cowboy movie on their computer in the bus station while waiting for the bus. The Sufi saw a cowboy loaded with guns and other things walking in the Wild West, waiting to be challenged. The Sufi said to himself, "Wow, this is like walking with *wudhu*- loaded with the Qur'an on the right side of your jacket pocket, and *dua*/prayer/litany book on the left side of your jacket pocket, having *tasbih* on the right side of your pants and having *athar*/scent on the left side of your pants."

IN PRACTICE

To be loaded spiritually can be the readiness and constant fulfilling of one's daily award, regular chants/*dhikr*/prayers. At any time, an evil can come and hit the person. If the person is not loaded spiritually, he or she may easily die. In practice, one does not challenge and ask for evil but always asks from Allah ﷻ easiness, blessings, and protection from the evil-seeming incidents. Yet, if it comes as a test, trial, or for any other purpose, then the person should be ready to take care of it.

86. Remembrance

The Sufi used to go to the Boston airport for work every Wednesday. The Sufi used to get a cup of hot water to make her own coffee with chants from a coffee shop at the airport. There was a cute Chinese bartender. Each time the Sufi went and offered money, she used to say, "That is okay. No money needed." The airport was extremely busy every day with thousands of people. After a few weeks, the Sufi went again on a Wednesday. She asked again for a cup of hot water and tried to hand over the credit card as usual although the bartender did not charge any money. This time the bartender said, "We can't give you this for free every day," but still she did not charge for the hot water. The Sufi smiled and left and said to herself, "The importance of regular prayers!"

In practice

It is important to practice the prayers and rituals regularly. Allah ﷻ accepts and gives the reward of prayers as if the person spent in one worship to another with the Divine Mercy and Grace. In the above story, although the Sufi went to the coffee shop every Wednesday, the bartender thought that she was coming every day due to the regularity. On a positive note, she remembered her among hundreds of people visiting the coffee shop.

87.   The Man of Gratitude

The Sufi used to know a man for many years. He always used to say, "Alhamdulillah" or "Many thanks and all gratitude[8] is to Allah ﷻ." One day, this man had a big accident and he was about to die. The Sufi saw the man. The man said to the Sufi, "Many thanks and gratitude to Allah ﷻ." After a year, the Sufi saw this man again. He had brain surgery. He was almost going to die due internal bleeding in his head. The man said to the Sufi, "Many thanks and gratitude to Allah ﷻ." After a few more years, the man got older. The Sufi saw the man again. The man had a stroke and he was hardly able to talk. The few words that the man was able to utter to the Sufi were, "Many thanks and all the gratitude to Allah ﷻ." The Sufi started crying on the spot!

In practice

It is important to embody thankfulness, gratitude and appreciation to Allah ﷻ. This life is a test to reveal the levels of people in their degree of gratitude of Allah ﷻ. Some of us can complain with a small pin pain on our body due to an accident and immediately blame Allah ﷻ questioning why Allah ﷻ did not protect us. Some exceptional people like the man in the above story can embody gratitude and thankfulness for Allah ﷻ. Allah ﷻ appreciates and prepares great rewards for the ones who excel in this test of recognition and remain always grateful to Allah ﷻ.

---

8. Shukr in Arabic.

88.   Leaving the Present and Forgetfulness

One day, the Sufi was enjoying his presence with Allah ﷻ. Then, he forgot that he was teaching class. His phone was receiving texts from the students. He still did not understand why he was receiving texts. He continued his presence. After a while, when the class time was over, he remembered that he had a class that day. He called the students and apologized to them and said to himself, "It should be the case of full presence."

In practice

It is important to aim to be in the full presence[ix] of Allah ﷻ constantly. This state can sometimes entail forgetting everything except fully embodying being in the presence of Allah ﷻ. It may sometimes be difficult to transform from these spiritual states into humanly expected engagements and responsibilities.

89.   Reminders & Blame

There was a Sufi who used to remind people before bad things happened so that people could do something to fix the issues before they happened. When a problem already happened, the Sufi used to not remind but rather try to console the people and make them feel easy. A friend of hers asked, "Why don't you remind them that you told them before about the possible problems?" The Sufi said, "If I tell after the problem occurs, then it is called blame, but not a reminder. The reminder is the advice before something happens so that people can take some precautions."

In practice

Rasulullah ﷺ Muhammad never did blame people when people did not listen to his advice. He instructed them with reminders before but afterwards he did not blame them. There are many incidents of this principle. There were even cases[x] when people faced very dire outcomes due to not listening the Prophet. After the incident, Rasulullah ﷺ did not say even once, "I told you but you didn't listen." In every aspect of life, our role models such as Rasulullah ﷺ teach us how to be a real human being without breaking people's hearts.

90. The Double Man

One day, there was a very pious Sufi sitting in a gathering with a very pious teacher. As he was sitting silently and with his eyes closed benefiting from the presence of this pious teacher, the Sufi for just a second opened his eyes and saw across from him his exact copy sitting in the same gathering. The Sufi was startled seeing exact his copy in front of him. Then, he started thinking about it.

IN PRACTICE

Allah SWT sometimes sends angels to encourage the person in their genuine and sincere efforts for Allah ﷻ. Sometimes the angels can visit the person in the human form to test the person whether the person is on the path of Allah ﷻ genuinely or not.

91. Real Sincerity & Fame

There was a writer Sufi. One day, the writer Sufi met another Sufi who was in practice. This new Sufi had a very interesting life story of change. He tried different ways of spirituality before becoming a Sufi. This Sufi said to the writer Sufi, "You can write my life story. Maybe, it may inspire others. In case it becomes famous and one of the top reads, I don't want to be known. Please don't use my name or any identifiers so that in case people want to backtrack to me, they won't figure out that it is my biography."

IN PRACTICE

Sincerity, *ikhlas*, is the key. Everything is performed to please Allah SWT. All the efforts of inspiration are performed to please Allah SWT. In this case, fame in the efforts of inspiring others can be poisonous. The natural human tendency can be eagerness to become famous to inspire others in order to please Allah ﷻ. Yet, this can be one of the traps on the path. To avoid this trap, the person should really seek and ask, "How can I be unknown by all humans and known only by Allah ﷻ, and yet inspire others towards goodness?" This is the real sincerity, *ikhlas*. Humanly recognitions, titles, and fame are valueless and even they can be a spiritual poison for the person. Unidentified, unnamed, and unknown engagements by humans are spiritually safer and more sincere than their opposite that attract other lowly intentions and motivations.

92.   The Crying, the Mother and the Sufi

One day, there was a Sufi who visited his mom. He mentioned to his mom about the genuine practice. His mom got angry and cursed his teachers. The Sufi started crying and went to his teacher and explained what happened. The Sufi asked his teacher if he could pray for his mom. Then the teacher started praying for her. Then, the Sufi went to his home. He knocked on the door. The mom opened the door and apologized about what she did. She said, "Can you please teach me the spiritual practice? I need it in my life."

In practice

The prayers of teachers for the students are very effective. Allah ﷻ can easily answer these prayers compared to other relationships. There is no interest-based relationship between the teacher and student. In the genuine practice, they engage with their roles of teaching and learning in order to please Allah ﷻ.

93.   The Man of Astagfirullah

One day, the Sufi was traveling to Toronto, Canada. He stopped by a mosque to pray. A man from elsewhere led the prayer but not the imam. After the prayer, the man said from nowhere, "Please make abundance of *astagfirullah* and don't be angry." The Sufi said to himself, "He is talking to me."

In practice

Allah can inspire people and even send angels in the form of humans to address their dilemma if they are trying on the path of Allah ﷻ sincerely and trying to be aware of their inner voices or dialogues. It is not uncommon in the tradition that individuals show up from nowhere to address the need of a person. It is not uncommon in the tradition that the teachers or friends of Allah SWT address from nowhere the problems of the person in a lecture. Yet, one should take heed of it and change oneself and appreciate the One constantly Who sends these reminders.

94.   The Wise Fool and the Locked Doors

There was a wise fool who used to sometimes act as a fool and sometimes as wise. When he used to act wisely, people let him enter the mosque. When he used to act foolishly, people did not let him enter the mosque. The Sufi was observing this incident. Each time the wise fool was on probation of not entering the mosque due to his foolishness, he used to come to the mosque and the mosque door would be locked. The Sufi was inside by himself in the mosque. Each time, the wise fool used to come to the locked doors. Sometimes he opened them although the wise fool did not have the keys for these doors. The Sufi at first used to get startled about it while observing this, but then he tried to normalize it and tried to understand the wisdom behind it.

In practice

The people who are loved by Allah SWT are hidden. It is very critical not to treat any person harshly and break their hearts. Especially, if they are loved by Allah ﷻ, then the person may take the risk of attracting the displeasure of Allah SWT on oneself. This can be very dangerous even this person who causes uneasiness for others is another Friend of Allah ﷻ. Another point is that the places of worship are venues for people to discharge themselves and connect with Allah ﷻ. We don't have authority to ban people from entering these places. In the above story, the wise-fool was a hidden person perhaps loved by Allah ﷻ. Allah ﷻ enabled him to enter this place of worship beyond physical means.

95. Sufi and Escalator

One day, the Sufi used the escalator to go down. She remembered that she forgot to take something from her room. She ran back against the opposite moving direction of the escalator. Then, she fell down and hurt her hand. Then, she said to herself, "My sins." She immediately went to the room asking forgiveness from Allah ﷻ.

In Practice

Nothing happens randomly. One's own thoughts and actions can be the cause of one's evil rendering toward their own selves to oppress themselves. Therefore, one should not blame anyone but immediately rush in solitude to ask forgiveness and help from Allah ﷻ.

96.   Injury and the Sufi

One day, the Sufi fell down and hurt her hand. She was thinking about the possible meanings behind this injury. She asked for forgiveness from Allah ﷻ and asked for protection from the possible expected renderings in the destiny.

IN PRACTICE

It is important to realize that nothing happens randomly. There are apparent, external and internal meanings to every occurrence. The person can ask protection from the possible outcomes of an incident from its internal meanings. Allah ﷻ can change anything. Allah ﷻ can transform an expected bad outcome to a positive outcome if one turns to Allah ﷻ, makes repentance and asks forgiveness with humility and sincerity.

97. The Sleeping Man in the Kitchen

One day, the Sufi went to the mosque to pray the morning prayer at 6:45 am. After 10 minutes of prayer, everyone left except the Sufi. The Sufi stayed in the mosque for a few hours to do his work. It was peaceful and silent in the mosque. After working for a few hours, the Sufi wanted to go to the kitchen to get a cup to make coffee. The kitchen door was locked. This was unusual. As he was walking around the kitchen door, he heard a noise from the kitchen and the door suddenly opened. The Sufi was startled and said, *"A'uzu billahi min asshaytani rajim."* A man came out from the kitchen and said, " I fell asleep while waiting for my bus." The Sufi said, *"Assalumu Alaykum."* The man said, *"Alaykum Assalam."*

In practice

It is important to always ask refuge in Allah ﷻ from unexpected incidents or events. There are seen or unseen beings that we may realize or not. Yet, we can constantly make the protection prayers as taught by Rasulullah ﷺ Muhammad saw in order to take refuge in Allah ﷻ from everything.

98.   The Best Time for Prayer

One day, the Sufi was looking for a best time to pray to Allah ﷻ. As he was constantly searching for this best time, he realized that he has been not doing any prayers, but only thinking about this. He said to himself, "The best time is when you immediately remember to make prayer."

IN PRACTICE

It is important to optimize the results and expectations from Allah ﷻ by selecting the best time for prayers. Rasulullah ﷺ Muhammad saw kept his special prayer for humans after death on the Judgment Day. All other prophets and messengers of Allah ﷻ used their prayer for their people and followers in this world. Yet, if one would be affected with the whispers of laziness and heedlessness in the effort of searching for the best time and therefore not pray to Allah ﷻ, then he or she should pray immediately as he or she feels the need for it.

99. Sharing and Caring: Food

There was a Sufi who had four kids. One of the kids did not want to share his food but if someone ate his food secretly he did not care. Another kid did like to share his food but if someone ate her food secretly, she got very angry and started screaming. There was another kid who did not like to share her food and became extremely angry when someone ate her food secretly. There was another kid who did like to share his food and did not care if someone ate his food secretly. The Sufi loved the last one the most and said to herself, "I wish even some adults can be like him, a very good quality. MashAllah!"

In practice

Our real character reveals itself when we are tested with the application of these sublime teachings on the path of Allah ﷻ. There are a lot of people who preach and listen to preachers and even cry. Yet, when it comes to application they are not really aware of their own selves.

100. Oatmeal and Capacity

One day, the Sufi was making oatmeal. He put some hot water on the oatmeal. The oatmeal started sucking in the water and started becoming big. The Sufi was amazed with this oatmeal. The Sufi had a little bit of hot water left in the boiler. He said to himself, "Let me add this as well, so that the oatmeal can get bigger and this remaining hot water is not wasted." He added it and after waiting half an hour, the oatmeal did not suck in the extra water. The Sufi said to himself, "Everything has a capacity!"

IN PRACTICE

Knowledge and experience depends on the capacity of the person. Sometimes, giving more than what is needed may not have much use but it may affect the texture and quality negatively. One can always ask from Allah ﷻ to increase one's capacity in spiritual engagements and knowledge in order to please Allah ﷻ.

101. Galaxies and the Person

One day, the Sufi attended a gathering. There was an attendee who was discussing the galaxies. There was another attended who disagreed with the argument and she emphasized the importance of the self in one's own inner journey rather than the outer journeys of spiritual traveling. The teacher was watching the conversation and said, "Both are important to break the attitude of heedlessness and 'I don't care' for different people. It can also be important for the same person who may be going through different conditions with different spiritual states."

In practice

It is important to recognize the different avenues given by Allah ﷻ to break our attitudes of unrecognition and unappreciation in our relationships with the Divine. Sometimes, the realization of stars, the moon, and galaxies and sometimes a feeling coming from simple human engagement can help the person to break this heedlessness. A person in different states of spiritual engagement can benefit from each at different times. Different people with different spiritual tastes of engagements can benefit differently from each of the available resources.

102. Troubles and Meanings

One day, the Sufi woke up and she had a headache. As usual, she started her day with her normal schedule. She started with her *dhikr*, meditation, and recitations of the scripture. As she was preparing to go to work, she thought, "I hope it is a fast and routine day as usual that passes quickly because my mind is all over the place and I cannot collect myself mentally and emotionally. I also have headache." With these thoughts, she went to her work. At work, she found herself in the middle of a mess with people blaming her about something. She was listening to the blames but did not have the energy to respond as her mental and emotional wanderings went further.

IN PRACTICE

It is important to constantly remember reliance on Allah ﷻ. Sometimes, our routines or normalizations make everything normal, implicitly assuming self-sufficiency but not dependency on Allah ﷻ. This can be called heedlessness[xi]. Yet, these moments of unexpected troubles, trials, or tests can pop up at any time and in any place. Our dispositions should be to seek forgiveness immediately from Allah ﷻ for any possible mistake on our part as David (PBUH) did as mentioned in the Scripture[xii]. As soon as two people in dispute appeared in front of him to resolve their issue, David (PBUH) gave his judgment. Yet, as soon they left, he immediately rushed to ask forgiveness from them due to the appearance of this unusual case as a sign of reminder from Allah ﷻ for him.

103. The Medical Practices of the Prophet

One day, the Sufi heard news about a spreading, deadly virus. The Sufi immediately engaged herself with both spiritual and medical practices as suggested by the Prophet. Then, she looked into the modern medical advice as suggested by the doctors.

In practice

The prophets receive divine guidance in the treatment of all spiritual and even bodily diseases. Therefore, one should first review the prophetic advice about prevention and treatment of diseases before seeking medical help from doctors. Both are means that Allah ﷻ enables and Allah ﷻ gives both the cure and treatment for diseases. One should follow the means as a form of prayer and respect to Allah ﷻ. Laws and means are created by Allah ﷻ to be followed. Therefore, medicine is a science as the law of Allah ﷻ to be followed. Yet, one should always see them as means but not the real cause or effect. The Real Doer is Allah ﷻ behind all the means.

104. The Sufi and the Water Fountains

One day, the Sufi was traveling. He felt thirsty and stopped in a village. The village had a lot of water fountains for the travelers. As the Sufi entered the village he saw these different water fountains with different designs made for the travelers to quench their thirst without any payment. The Sufi went to one water fountain. He tasted the water. He said, "This tastes excellent and pure." Then, he said to himself, "I want to taste all the water from all of the different fountains." Then, he started trying all of them. He said, "SubhanAllah! They all taste the same-excellent and pure! Their source should be the same."

In practice

Allah SWT sends at different times different scriptures and prophets to all humans to remind them of their meaning, goal, and purpose in life. The commonalities of these teachings show that the Source is the same. We may refer to Allah SWT, Adonai, Allah ﷻ, the One, or other Beautiful Names and Attributes. The differences and contradictions may indicate impurity or human additions or alterations into the original, pure, authentic source.

105. Positive Group Association

One day, the Sufi was thinking, "Why do I take so much pleasure if I am involved and associated with doing something good although Allah SWT does not need it from me?" He was thinking about the answer to this question for many years. Then, one Friday morning, when he was doing his regular engagement with the Qur'ān, he had a little bit sparkling in his mind about this throbbing question and said, "If I claim that good thing is from me, then it will be arrogance. If I deny it, then it can be ingratitude or a lie. If I say *Alhamdulillah* and accept being part of it although it can be just a miniscule effort, then my association with it gives me joy, positive assurance and certitude on the path of Allah SWT."

IN PRACTICE

Real enablement of all the good things are from Allah ﷻ, the One, Allah SWT. Yet, we may not know how to act when we realize these constant bounties showering on us. Allah SWT does not need any of these good deeds of ours. Yet, inclination for good work by using our free will gives us solace, calm, peace, positivity, and happy perspectives in life. Therefore, it is an honor to be used as a small insignificant tool on the path of Allah ﷻ by doing good and virtuous acts. These acts are not our achievements but given to us as a Grace from Allah ﷻ. Therefore, we say *Alhamdulillah* with gratitude for Allah ﷻ to be the simple means but do not claim any of those achievements to be ours.

106. Spending Time with the Dead

One day, the Sufi visited Medina. Everyone in the tour group was saying, "*Alhamdulillah*, let's spend some time with Rasulullah ﷺ saw." There was a novice person in the group. He said, "How can we spend time with *Rasulullah* ﷺ? He is not alive, but he is in his grave." The Sufi smiled and said, "Just spend a few days sitting and making your *dhikr* in *masjid* Nabawi next to the blessed grave of *Rasulullah* ﷺ, then you will understand." A few days later, the novice man said to the Sufi, "Now, I understand!"

IN PRACTICE

Death is nothing but death of the body, not the soul. When there is a person next to a grave, there is the interaction of the souls. When a person spends a little time next to the Highest Soul, Rasulullah ﷺ ﷺ, then there are the effects of this communication, presence, and interaction showering upon the person from Rasulullah ﷺ saw with the permission of Allah SWT. If the person cannot visit the Prophet, similar effects from Rasulullah ﷺ can come to the person with *Salawat* with the permission of Allah SWT every day, especially on Fridays.

107. Humanness of Rasulullah ﷺ (Saw)

One day, the Sufi was thinking about Rasulullah ﷺ (saw). She said to herself, "What is the most unique feature of Rasulullah ﷺ saw?" She exclaimed, "His humanness!"

In practice

Allah ﷻ sends us prophets as humans as we are humans. Yet, the prophets are role models to show us how to be a real human being as our expected goal, purpose, and meaning in life is to please Allah ﷻ. All the prophets including Rasulullah ﷺ eat, drink, go to the marketplace and get married to normalize our human needs. Yet, at the same time as narrated in the Qur'ăn, they show us how to balance the life of a human with high goals, fulfilling intention and rewarding purpose to be happy and content in this life and after death. When one analyzes the life of Rasulullah ﷺ saw, one can be mesmerized with these human qualities of Rasulullah ﷺ saw with balance and the middle-way of kindness, gentleness, and care. Yet, at the same time, his spiritual level is higher than the angels.

108. The Sufi teacher of the Bird

Every day, as the Sufi was leaving the mosque, a bird used to approach the Sufi and stare at his face. Then, the Sufi took a moment to read to the bird from the verses of the Qur'ān on the hoopoe and Rasulullah ﷺ Solomon. The bird used to carefully listen and fully focus without any chirping and come closer and closer to the Sufi as he was reading. Each day, after the Sufi finished the recitation of the Qur'ān, he said to the bird, "Assalamu alaykum, peace be upon you," and left walking to his car. The bird tried to escort the Sufi as much as possible to his car.

IN PRACTICE

It is important to have a relationship of *adab* between the student and teacher. *Adab* can be translated as the etiquettes of respect. Some of these etiquettes of the student of knowledge is to be always ready, wait, and be prepared for your teacher with *adab* and respect. The student should work around the schedule of the teacher but not the opposite. When the teacher starts teaching, to give full attention to the teacher is another *adab*. When the teacher finishes the teaching, to escort the teacher when they are leaving with *adab,* respect and humbleness are some of these etiquettes. Animals can follow these etiquettes as mentioned in the above story. How about humans?

109. The Absent Student: The Bird

The Sufi used to teach a bird about the conversation of the hoopoe and Rasulullah ﷺ Solomon in the Qur'ān. Each time the Sufi used to leave the mosque, the bird used to come respectfully with *adab,* taking his lesson and then leave. One day, the Sufi did not see the bird attending the class. Then, he tried to look for the bird and was concerned about him. After some time looking for the bird, the Sufi said to himself, "I tried to do my part as a teacher."

IN PRACTICE

The teachers have a responsibility to look after their students. If the student is sick or if they are in need, the teacher should try to do their best to ask about them, help, and fulfill their needs. In the above story, when the Sufi did not find the bird attending the class, he was worried about the bird and put in an effort to look for him.

110. Good Company

One day, the Sufi was thinking about the reason for her fears, uneasiness, and feelings of insecurity. She was thinking about this for a long time. Then, she visited some good friends. They did a group chant and reading. The Sufi felt super happy, calm, and refreshed. All of her fears were gone. She said to herself, "My need for good company!"

IN PRACTICE

It is very critical to be around good company of friends and teachers from whom the person can benefit from their experiential knowledge on the path of Allah ﷻ. A person can be a genius, a good reader, and a critical thinker. Yet, a human is a human. They need good people to receive different frequencies of goodness from their experience.

111. Dual Identities

There was a Sufi who used to immediately detect the ill feelings in himself towards others. One day, he felt the feelings of jealousy[9] towards some people. He immediately caught it and started the work, struggle, and process of terminating these feelings and transforming them into better and positive ones. Another day, a person came to the Sufi and praised him about how great he was. Then, the Sufi immediately caught his feelings of conceit, vanity, and arrogance. He then immediately engaged in the self-struggle of terminating them and transforming them into more positive ones. The Sufi was really getting tired from these constant struggles of the fight within himself between dual identities.

IN PRACTICE

The purpose of life is the struggle between the pure identity of soul as created by Allah ﷻ and raw ego, *nafs* which is pumped up falsely by Satan and with which we are constantly deceived. The struggle is to train this raw ego referred to as *nafs*. The soul should be decision maker but not the *nafs*. The purpose of existence is the life-long struggle between the soul and *nafs*. In this struggle, Allah ﷻ is All Merciful. Allah ﷻ sent us the Qurān, Rasulullah ﷺ ﷺ and all the other messengers as guidance and role models for us to define the nature of this struggle and how to win the game.

---

9. Hasad in Ar.

112. Assumptions & Laws

One day, the Sufi traveled to another country to visit his friend. The laws and norms of the country were different than the norms and laws in his home country. The Sufi was surprised how the laws were so detailed and different in this country, and asked his friend, "Why are the norms and laws in this country so very different than my home country?" His friend said, "In some societies, the norms and, accordingly, the laws assume that humans are good, ethical, and moral and accordingly, expect initiatives from people. In some societies, the norms and, accordingly, the laws assume that humans are evil, bad, and oppressive and accordingly, protects people from their harms."

In practice

Contrasting and comparing different cultures and norms can make a person judgmental about the practices of others. Rasulullah ﷺ ﷺ was never judgmental about other cultures, norms, and teachings. There was an influx of different people from different cultures, understandings, and norms accepting the teachings of Rasulullah ﷺ ﷺ. Yet, he accepted them as they were and taught them the means to connect with Allah ﷻ through worship, meditation, practices of individual rights, and justice.

113. The Squirrel and the Sufi

One day, the Sufi was taking a walk in the early morning and reading his regular routine from the scripture. As he was walking, there was a squirrel standing in the Sufi's path and eating a nut while looking at the Sufi. The Sufi started staring at the squirrel. The squirrel was eating and looking at the Sufi as well. The Sufi said to himself, "We are both connected with *imān* and *dhikr*. Therefore, the squirrel is my friend. We have the same goal."

IN PRACTICE

Everything chants, praises, and prays to Allah ﷻ in its own language. The perspective of *imān*, faith or belief in One Creator, Allah ﷻ, Adonai, or Allah ﷻ gives a positive meaning to all of creation and to everything in the universe. In this sense, nothing is scary compared to the philosophies not emphasizing *imān*. In these worldviews, everything becomes scary because there is a disconnect among everything. There is no structure, system, a positive hierarchy. In these gloomy perspectives, everything is in chaos, fighting for their rights, freedom. Everything is enemy to each other. The powerful abuse the weak. Therefore, the weak are doomed to disappear due to so-called 'natural selection'. One has a choice in life-either continue with these 'assumptions of darkness' worldviews which increase one's depression; or embrace all of the creation with purpose, meaning, and friendship as the servants of Allah ﷻ.

114. Modern Slaves

One day, the Sufi traveled to another town to visit her doctor friend. They were very happy to see each other. Although the Sufi was with the doctor, the doctor was constantly on her phone- sometimes talking or texting to her patients, or shopping, or engaging herself with social media in different chat groups. The Sufi felt uncomfortable. Although her friend was there physically, her mind and emotional states were not present. The doctor constantly had her head down looking at her phone while walking in the house and while outside. The Sufi felt bad about her friend. Yet, she seemed to be happy and not care about her engagements.

In practice

Mental and emotional slavery can be worse than physical notions of slavery. Our modern slavery hides behind the popular terms of liberty and freedom. Yet, we don't have any self-focus times to engage ourselves with self-accountability. Self-engagements in focus take the person for self-discoveries. True self-discoveries lead the person to Allah ﷻ with the reality of *La ilaha illa Allah*. Modern slavery instigates a spiritual disease that 'the world is rotating around me'. This can mean that 'I am so important that if something happens to me everything is going to collapse.' Yet, Allah ﷻ mentions in the Qurãn often the mortality of all great humans indicating fully the reality of our upcoming demise. Intelligent is the person who focuses on *La ilaha illa Allah*.

115. Self-Destructive Group Identities

One day, the Sufi attended a gathering to benefit herself about collective engagements of spirituality. The lecturer was constantly giving examples of the greatness of her spiritual school. The Sufi felt uncomfortable.

IN PRACTICE

Group identities on the spiritual path should come with balance. A person can claim or say, "My group is the best, but it is not the only way." Considering one's spiritual path as the best is normal and expected, so that the person can follow the guidelines on that path from a teacher. Yet, it is wrong to assume and say, "My group is the ONLY way." This implies arrogance, falsehood, and deviation from the true path of Allah ﷻ.

116. The Old Man and the Sufi

There was a man who spent almost all his life in evil and bad actions. As he was becoming very old, approaching ninety years old, one day, he met with the Sufi. The Sufi and the old man became good friends. As the old man was spending time with the Sufi, he started leaving his bad habits and wanted to learn more and more on the path. One day, the Sufi received a call from the old man. The old man was crying on the phone. He said, "Please come and pick me up, I can't drive due to my old age. Please take me to one of these chanting sessions." The Sufi felt so bad for the old man and went to pick up the old man. After picking up the old man, the Sufi was driving the car to their place of gathering for chanting. Then, while they were waiting at a red light, the Sufi said something about the angel of death and he immediately heard a big bang. The Sufi did not understand what was happening and fainted on the spot in the car. After a few minutes, he woke up to an ambulance, police car, and firetruck sirens. The Sufi and the old man were in a big car incident. They were hit from the side while waiting at the red light. The old man was dead in his seat in the car as he was holding on his lap, the book of chant.

IN PRACTICE

Allah ﷻ values everyone's effort on the Divine path until the last minute before death. We don't know how, where, and when we will die. Yet, the way of ending is very critical. The way of ending life can be an indication how we would be welcomed or not for the next life. Therefore, a true person on the path should always be ready for the departure at any time and anywhere. The old man did not seem to live in piety for most of his life. Yet, his effort and genuine intention seemed to put him in a position to end his life on the Divine path.

117. The Mechanic & The Professor

One day, the Harvard Sufi went to a fast food place with his kids since it was Friday and the end of their school week. All of the kids were very happy to eat a nice and yummy chicken hoagie. As they were jumping around in the restaurant and impatiently awaiting their hoagies, there was a Sufi from Yemen eating his own food. The two Sufis did not know each other. While eating, the Yemeni Sufi was chatting with the Harvard Sufi's kids and mentioned that he was a mechanic and fixing the cars. The Harvard Sufi was checking to see if he parked okay on the street, going back and forth watching outside so that he didn't get a ticket. The Yemeni Sufi finished his food and called over to the Sufi and said, "Please, I want to pay for your food." The Sufi said, "No, that is ok, thank you." The Yemeni Sufi insisted so much and the Harvard Sufi accepted it. Then, the Harvard Sufi went to his car and got an expensive gift and gave it to the Yemeni Sufi. The kids were watching all this. They were amazed and asking questions to understand what was happening. The Harvard Sufi said to himself, "Throw the titles, Harvard, Phds and MDs in the garbage! Be a real man like this person!"

IN PRACTICE

It is very important to be generous. One of the cultures known for their trait of generosity is Yemen. Rasulullah ﷺ had a special praise for the people of Yemen. Rasulullah ﷺ highly encourages exchanging gifts, feeding each other and being generous so that there is the increase of love between brothers and sisters. In practice, it is important to embody the traits than the titles. There are a lot of unknown and secret people called *ahlullah*, loved by Allah ﷻ. This is the real status and title.

118. Cupping and Going to ER

There were two friends in the mosque. One was trained in cupping. He used to do cupping on people. The other friend used to watch his expert friend while he was cupping others. The expert cupper needed to relocate to another town. One day, an old man came to the mosque and said, "I am looking for the expert cupper. I have a lot of back pain." The cupper's friend was there and said, "He moved from here. If you want, I can do it for you. It is not difficult." During the cupping, there was heavy bleeding. The ambulance came and took the old man to the hospital's emergency room. He almost died.

In practice

It is important to genuinely learn and apply the spiritual teachings under the guidance and mentor of a teacher. Sometimes, we cause spiritual deaths on others and on ourselves but we don't realize it.

119. Wishing "Peace" for Everyone

There was a Sufi who used to say, "Peace upon you" to whomever she used to meet. One day, she met another Sufi and she said, "Why do you always say 'peace upon you' to everyone? We only say it to our role models." The other Sufi said, "Why do you want to limit the peace coming from Allah ﷻ to only certain people? Allah's peace is infinite."

IN PRACTICE

Some people may be confused when a person says "peace upon this person" if he or she is not one of the role models such as prophets or messengers. These are terminologies to differentiate among the most elect, the elect, and the pious. For example (PBUH) as "as" for the prophets or messengers, may Allah ﷻ be pleased with them as "ra" and may Allah ﷻ have mercy on them as "rh." All are good.

120. Simple Is Better

There was a Turkish Sufi married to an American Sufi. One day, the Turkish Sufi was at home with her kids. She made macaroni for her children and made it in Turkish style with mint, diced tomatoes, olive oil and salt. After that she served it to the kids. All the kids were asking for ketchup and hot sauce. The Sufi insisted that they needed to eat in the way that she made it with her style. The kids started crying and said, "If our dad was here, he would give us whatever we want. We don't want to eat plain macaroni." The Sufi said, "Either you eat it this way, or no food!" After the kids ate the food, they started saying among themselves, "Wow! This is the best macaroni we have ever eaten although it looked plain and it was much healthier!"

IN PRACTICE

Sometimes, we cry and ask something from Allah ﷻ in such a way that we are very confident about our position. In the end, we got disturbed, and ungrateful in our relationship with Allah ﷻ because the result was not in the way that we wanted. After many years, we start seeing the benefits of Allah ﷻ-given results over the ones we deemed good and desired to have. Then, at that point in time, if we haven't lost our sense of gratitude, we apologize to and ask forgiveness from Allah ﷻ. But, all those years between the disconnection from to the re-connection with Allah ﷻ could have been wasted in misery and darkness. Yet, if we develop the attitude of gratitude and constant reliance on Allah ﷻ, all the years, months, days and even minutes can be spent in constant sweetness and tranquility.

Discussion Questions

- ▸ Discuss a time when something worked out better than you had expected and you looked back at the time spent worrying and knew you had wasted that time feeling that way. How do you wish you would have spent that time instead?

▶ Was there ever something in life you really wanted only to find out later that it wasn't as good for you as you thought it was going to be?

▶ Have you grown to appreciate something in your life for becoming more than you expected it to be when it first came into your life?

▶ Have you had any experiences of feeling like you received just what you needed, right when you needed it, even if it wasn't exactly what you would have preferred?

▶ Have you ever had the experience of feeling, "That's just what I needed!" after something has happened to help take care of you, make your day better, or nurture you in some way that you didn't even know you needed until after it happened?

▶ How have these experiences affected your sense of gratitude to Allah ﷻ and faith in Allah ﷻ?

ENDNOTES

i. Sunnah & Hadith
ii. The teachings of the Qurān and Sunnah
iii. Jawamul Kalim
iv. Tawakkul
v. Taslim
vi. Gaflah
vii. The Qurān [38:24]
viii. Miraj
ix. Khudur
x. The Prophet's suggestion about Uhud.
xi. Gaflah
xii. The Qurān [38:24]

BIBLIOGRAPHY

[1] Al-Ghazzali, M. *Al-Ghazzali on Knowing Yourself and Allah* ﷻ. Kazi Publications Inc., 2003.

[2] Vahide, S. *The Collection of Light*. ihlas nur publication, 2001.

[3] al-Ba'uniyyah, A. *The Principles of Sufism*. NYU Press, 2016.

[4] Kumek, Y. J. *Practical Mysticism: Sufi Journeys of Heart and Mind*. Kendall Hunt, 2018.

[5] Muslim, A. *Sahih Muslim*, translated by A. Siddiqui. Peace Vision. 1972.

[6] Al-Bukhari, M. *The Translation of the Meanings of Sahih Al-Bukhari*. Kazi Publications, 1986.

[7] Ozkan, T. Y. *A Muslim Response to Evil: S. N. on the Theodicy*. Routledge, 2016.

[8] Murad, K. *In The Early Hours: Reflections on Spiritual and Self Development*. Kube Publishing Ltd, 2013.

[9] U. P. Oxford, "Oxford Dictionaries," 2016, http://www.oxforddictionaries.com/us/definition/american_english/.

[10] Al-Ghazali, M. *Deliverance from Error*. Louisville: Fons Vitae, 2000.

[11] Ali, A. Y. *The Meaning of the Glorious Qurān*. Islamic Books, 1938.

[12] Dawud, A. *Sunan Abu Dawud*. Darussalam, 2008.

[13] Ashraf, M. M. K. 'Alī Thānvī, *The Path to Perfection: An Edited Anthology of the Spiritual Teachings of Hakīm Al-Umma Mawlānā Ashraf 'Alī Thānawī*. White Thread, 2005.

[14] Ibn Qayyim. I. K. *The Soul's Journey After Death*. Noah, 2018.

[15] Vandestra, M. *Human Souls Journey After Death In Islam*. Dragon Promedia, 2017.

[16] Hanbal, A. B. *Musnad Imam Ahmad Ibn Hanbal*. Dar-Us-Salam Publications, 2012.

[17] U. P. Oxford, "Oxford Dictionaries," 2016. [Online]. Available: http://www.oxforddictionaries.com/us/definition/american_english/.

[18] Al-Ghazali, M. *Deliverance from Error,* Louisville: Fons Vitae, 2000.

[19] Salamah-Qudsi, A. *Sufism and Early Islamic Piety: Personal and Communal Dynamics.* Cambridge University Press, 2018.

[20] Muslim, A. *Sahih Muslim* (translated by Siddiqui, A.). Peace Vision. 1972.

[21] Hanbal, A. B. *Musnad Imam Ahmad Ibn Hanbal.* Dar-Us-Salam Publications, 2012.

[22] Kumek, Y. J. *Practical Mysticism: Sufi Journeys of Heart and Mind.* Kendall Hunt, 2018.

[23] Ansar, A. *Peace of Mind and Healing Broken Lives.* Universal Mercy, 2010.

[24] Smith, J. I. and Y. Y. Haddad. *The Islamic Understanding of Death and Resurrection.* Oxford University Press, 2002.

[25] Dorothy, G. and J. L. Singer. *Handbook of Children and the Media.* SAGE, 2002.

[26] Ring, N.C. *Introduction to the Study of Religion.* New York: Orbis, 2007.

[27] Ozkan, T. Y. *A Muslim Response to Evil: S. N. on the Theodicy.* Routledge, 2016.

[28] Al-Bukhari, M. *The Translation of the Meanings of Sahih Al-Bukhari.* Kazi Publications, 1986.

[29] Al-Ansari, A. B. "Ahadith al-Shuyukh al-Thiqat," vol. 2, no. 322, pp. 875–876.

[30] Tamer, Georges. *Islam and Rationality: The Impact of Al-Ghazālī: Papers Collected on His 900th Anniversary.* Boston: BRILL, 2015.

[31] Geoffroy, Eric, and Roger Gaetani. *Introduction to Sufism: The Inner Path of Islam.* Bloomington, Ind: World Wisdom, 2010.

[32] Shah, Idries. *The Sufis.* London: The Octagon Press, 1999.

[33] Jamal, Azim, and Nido R. Qubein. *Life Balance: The Sufi Way.* Mumbai, India: Jaico Pub. House, 2000.

[34] Shah, I. *Learning How to Learn: Psychology and Spirituality in the Sufi Way.* Octagon Press Ltd., 1978.

[35] Heer, Nicholas, Kenneth L. Honerkamp, al-Tirmidhī M. A. Hakīm, Muhammad -H. Sulamī, and Muhammad -H. Sulamī. *Three Early Sufi Texts.* Louisville: Fons Vitae, 2009.

[36] Singh, David E. *Sainthood and Revelatory Discourse: An Examination of the Bases for the Authority of Bayan in Mahwi Islam.* Delhi: Regnum International, 2003.

[37] Darimi, I. *Sunan Darimi.* Dar Al Kitab, 1997.

[38] Bukhari, M.I. I. *Moral Teachings of Islam: Prophetic Traditions from Al-Adab Al-mufrad.* Rowman Altamira, 2003.

[39] Schimmel, Annemarie, and Friedrich Heiler. *Deciphering the Signs of Allah ﷻ: A Phenomenological Approach to Islam ; [to the Memory of Friedrich Heiler (1892–1967)].* Albany: State Uni. of New York Press, 1994.

[40] Stowasser, Barbara F. *The Day Begins at Sunset: Perceptions of Time in the Islamic World.* I.B.Tauris, 2014.

[41] Al-Qahtani, S. B. W. *Fortress Of Muslim.* Darussalam Publishers, 2018.

[42] Abū, Dā'ūd S.-A.-S, and Ahmad Hasan. *Sunan Abu Dawud.* New Delhi: Kitab Bhavan, 2012.

[43] al-Qushayri, Abu -Q, and Alexander D. Knysh. *Al-qushayri's Epistle on Sufism: Al-risala Al-Qushayriyya Fi 'ilm Al-Tasawwuf.* Reading: Garnet Publishing, 2007.

[44] Ibn Qayyim, I. K. *The Soul's Journey After Death.* Noah, 2018.

[45] Khan, M. A. *Encyclopaedia of Sufism: Sufism and Naqshbandi order.* Anmol Publications, 2003.

[46] Adonis. *Sufism and Surrealism.* Saqi, 2013.

[47] Muhaiyaddeen, M R. B. *Dhikr: The Remembrance of Allah ﷻ.* Narbeth, Pa: Fellowship Press, 1999.

[48] Abdullah, P. M. *ISLAMIC TASAWWUF: Shariah And Tariqah.* Adam Publishers & Distributors, 2001.

[49] Vaughan-Lee, Llewellyn. *Love is a Fire: The Sufi's Mystical Journey Home.* The Golden Sufi Center, 2000.

[50] I. Majah, *Sunan Ibn Majah,* Kazi Publications, 1993.

[51] A. R. A. Nisa, *Sunan Nisai,* Kazi Publications, 1997.

[52] A. Muslim, Sahih Muslim (translated by Siddiqui, A.), *Peace Vision,* 1972.

[53] M. Tirmizi, Jami At-Tirmizi, *Dar-us-Salam,* 2007.

[54] M. Al-Bukhari, *The translation of the meanings of Sahih Al-Bukhari,* Kazi Publications, 1986.

[55] M. i. `. A. K. Al-Tabrizi, Mishkat al Masabih, Beirut: Dar Ibn Hazm, 2003.

[56] SInternational, *The Qurān,* Abul-Qasim Publishing House, 1997.

[57] S. Abu-Dawud, Sunan Abu Dawud, *Riyadh: Darussalam,* 2008.

GLOSSARY

A'bd: worshipper, servant, or slave

Accountability: liability, especially in Sufism and in Abrahamic traditions, everyone has a free will or agency in this world but accountability for their actions in the afterlife in front of Allah ﷻ

Adab: good manners, esp. in the relationship with Allah ﷻ in Sufism

Adjective: attribute, a phrase describing a noun

Adonai: name of Allah ﷻ in Judaism

Affair: relationship

Agency: acting as an agent or a carrier with free will

Alhamdulillah: a chanted divine phrase of appreciation of Allah ﷻ or Allah

Alienating: isolating, separating, disconnecting

Alienating Images of Allah ﷻ: understandings about Allah ﷻ that disconnects person to establish a regular relationship with the Divine or to follow a religion

Allah (ﷻ): Allah ﻰﻟﺎﻌﺗﻭ ﻪﻧﺎﺤﺒﺳ. The expression ﻰﻟﺎﻌﺗﻭ ﻪﻧﺎﺤﺒﺳ read as Subhānahu wa Tā'la also abbreviated as SWT and written as also Allah (SWT) is an expression of respect when the Name of Allah is mentioned. Among these expressions many English translations, one can be "Allah is One, Unique and Perfect with all the Divine Attributes and Names, far beyond human's negative and wrong constructions and imaginations. All Glory Belongs to Allah, the Most Exalted, the Most Respected, and the Most High."

Allude: explain, refer

Anger: uncontrolled and chaotic human spiritual state

Aphorism: sayings, proverbs in a culture, society, or belief

Appreciate: thank

Appreciative: with capital A, Allah ﷻ

Arabic: language, especially the language of revelation of the Qurān

Arrogance: feelings and actions of superiority

Ascension: rising, especially in Sufism increase of spiritual states in relationship with Allah ﷻ

Assert: claim

Astagfirullah: a divine phrase of asking forgiveness from Allah ﷻ and cleaning the heart

Attribute: adjective, a phrase describing a noun, especially in Sufism, attributes of Allah ﷻ: divine phrases describing Allah ﷻ

Authentic: original, genuine, true

Balance: modesty, especially in Sufism, following the middle way

Behavior: temporary nature of a person

Bismillah: a divine phrase of starting something with the blessing of Allah ﷻ

Book of Chant: the Qurān

Boost: increase

Bowing down: bending one's body, especially the act of respect by bending one's body, for Allah ﷻ

Candy: hard delight, especially in Sufism, the pleasures or miracles given to the person on the path of Allah ﷻ

Caution: carefulness, alertness, especially in Sufism, in spiritual manners not to be trapped by ego or self

Certainty: knowing without doubt, especially in Sufism, knowing and experiencing without doubt

Chanting: repeating, especially in Sufism, repeating the phrases with focus and experience

Chaos: disorder and confusion, especially in Sufism (spiritual) chaos being in negative states of anxiety, stress, and purposelessness

Charge: positive states of spirituality that makes the person happy, peaceful, and calm, especially in Sufism, filling oneself with divine knowledge and experience

Compassion: loving and caring

Confirming Book: the Qurãn

Confirming Scripture: the Qurãn

Conscience: internal instinct of distinguishing right or wrong

Consciousness: awareness

Constant: not changing, permanent, especially in practice, known as Reflective Attributes of Allah ﷻ, where humans have an image but Allah ﷻ has its source

Construction: formation of an abstract entity

Contract: squeeze

Convergence: similarity

Cookie: soft delight, small sweet cake, especially in Sufism, the pleasures or miracles given to the person on the path of Allah ﷻ

Cosmology: knowledge about the origin and development of the universe

Covenant: agreement

Death: end of physical faculties of a person, especially physical versus spiritual death; the soul does not die but the body dies in understanding of physical death in Islam

Dedication: sincere constant effort

Deity: representation of the transcendent

Detox: discharge

Devout: pious, practicing

Dhikr: as one of the names of the Qurãn, or any type of chant to remember Allah ﷻ

Discharge: negative states of spirituality that makes the person sad, stressed, and anxious, especially in Sufism, emptying oneself from all the temporal and worldly positive and negative attachments

Divine: transcendent

Doctrine: teaching

Dominance: control

Dream: visions when one is sleeping or awake

Ego: self, identifier of a person, especially in Sufism, raw and uneducated identifier and controller of a person

Elohim: name of Allah ﷻ in Judaism

Embodiment, versus embody: making it part of one's character

Endeavor: engagement, activities

Epistemology: theory of knowledge

Ethical: moral

Ethnographic: based on observation

Etiquette: good manners and respect, especially in Sufism, respect in the relationship with Allah ﷻ

Evil: anything that causes stress, sadness, or anxiety

Evil eye: the belief of unknown effects of the human eye across different cultures, traditions, and religions, especially in Sufism the evil eye effects due to extreme hatred, jealousy, or, oppositely, evil eye effects due to extreme veneration and love of someone

Expand: enlarge

Experience: internalization of knowledge

Experience or experiential knowledge: all types of learning except from a book or a teacher, internalizing and personalizing the formal learning

Figurative: unclear, secondary, and metaphorical

Free Will: free choice of a person in decision-making

Generous: with capital G, Allah ﷻ

Genre: type

Genuine: sincere, original, authentic

Ghazali: philosopher, theologician, Sufi mystic, lived in 12th century

Glorification: the mental, spiritual, and maybe verbal act of describing Allah ﷻ in an admirable way

Groundless: fake

Habitual: habit of doing something constantly

HasbiyaAllah: a chant with a meaning of "Allah ﷻ is sufficient for me"

Healthy Cookies: beneficial extraordinary incidents, such as miracles in Sufism

Heaven: a place of all maximized pleasures of bodily and spiritual engagements while being with Allah ﷻ

Hell: a place of punishment

Heretic: abnormal person, especially in Sufism, a desired state of being to experience and know the Divine

Humbleness: behavior of modesty in viewing oneself, especially in Sufism, accepting the weakness in one's relationship with Allah ﷻ and not being disrespectful and arrogant to Allah ﷻ

Humility: character or trait of humbleness

Illa Allah: "except Allah" or "except Allah ﷻ"

Images of Allah ﷻ: understandings and experiences about Allah ﷻ

Imitation: trying without real understanding

Infinite: Allah ﷻ, the Unlimited

Informant: a person who participates in anthropological research

InshAllah: Allah ﷻ willing, hopefully

Intention: planning ideas before the action

Internalize: making it part of one's character, trait, or nature in Sufism

Intrinsic: internal

Islam: name of a religion that emphasizes believing in one Allah ﷻ and Jesus, Moses, and Muhammad to be the human prophets of the Creator

Jihad: struggle, esp. spiritual struggle within oneself

Joseph: Prophet of Allah ﷻ in Islam, Christianity, and Judaism

Journey: struggles of following guidelines of a mystical school

Khidr: mystical being who is sent by Allah ﷻ at any time to help people in their problems; also believed to be the teacher of Moses in a mystical journey as mentioned in the Qurãn

Kitab: the Qurãn

Knowledge: theoretical understanding of something through education

La ilaha illa Allah: there is no Allah ﷻ except Allah, a critical Divine phrase of chanting in Sufism implying a spiritual charge and discharge

Literal: clear and primary

Lord: Allah ﷻ

Lucifer: Satan, mentioned in divine Qurãn such as the Bible and the Qurãn

Majnun: crazy or, especially in Sufism, heretic

Mantra: a repetitive phrase or sound, especially used in Hinduism and Buddhism

Meditation: deep focus especially with reflection

Memorization: learning by heart

Mercy: compassion and forgiveness

Middle way: living a balanced life in spiritual and worldly engagements

Mimic: imitate

Mind: logic, reason, and rationality

Miracle: incidents against the law of physics and against all natural sciences

Mosque: temple of Muslims

Muhammad: Rasulullah ﷺ of Islam, referred as "the Prophet" in the text

Musaddiq: the Qurãn

Mystic: a person who adopts the teachings of mysticism

Mysticism: the knowledge of the transcendent

Nafs: self in its raw form

Neat: tidy and in order

Negation: denial, esp. in Sufism, emptying from the mind and heart the imperfect ideas and feelings about Allah ﷻ

Neglectful: not giving the proper attention that is due

Notion: concept, idea

Ocean: a very large sea, especially in Sufism, represents Allah ﷻ the Unlimited or Allah ﷻ's Unlimited and Incomprehensible Knowledge

Odd: not even, unique, no equivalence

Olam: hidden, waiting to be discovered through experiential knowledge

One: with capital denoting the one and only Creator

Oppression: unjust action of the strong over the weak

Permanent: constant, not changing, not ending

Phenomenon: occurrence

Pious: devout, practicing

Poisonous Cookies: harmful extraordinary incidents, such as miracles in Sufism

Pollution: making something dirty

Popular culture: the ethnographic data gathered over the period of years among different Sufi communities

Preposition: a word that does not have a meaning by itself but has a meaning in relation to another word, especially in Sufism, prepositions having conceptual and terminological meanings when one describes the relationships with the Divine

Pronunciation: correct sounds of letters in a language

The Prophet: Rasulullah ﷺ *Muhammad (peace and blessings be upon him). The Arabic writing* ﷺ is read as "Sallahu alayhi wa salllam" abbreviated as "saws" when the name of Rasulullah ﷺ Muhammad is mentioned. The expressions ﷺ or saws are expressions and phrases of blessings and peace for Rasulullah ﷺ Muhammad. They are also the expressions and phrases of blessings and peace used for the other Prophets of Allah such as Abraham, Moses, and Jesus and others.

Prostration versus to prostrate: the act of respect by putting one's face on the ground, especially in Sufism, humbling oneself for Allah ﷻ by putting the face, the noble part of the body, on the ground

Qibla: the direction where Muslims and Sufis turn when they pray

Qurãn: sacred text of Muslims

Rabbinic: related with the Rabbis, the priests, and teachers of Judaism Recitation, versus to recite: reading versus to read

Rasulullah ﷺ: The word Rasulullah can be translated as "the Messenger or Prophet of Allah." Rasulullah in its usage is Rasulullah ﷺ *Muhammad (peace and blessings be upon him)* (PBUH). PBUH: *Peace and blessings be upon Him*

Reliance: dependence

Repetition: repeating

Reverence: respect

Reward: prize, payment, especially in worldly and afterlife rewards in Islam

Ritual: practices in a religion or mysticism that have spiritual and divine value for a person

Ruku: bowing down

Rumi: great Sufi mystic

Saint: the person believed to be close to Allah ﷻ

Sakina: peaceful and calm feelings

Salawat: names of the chants to remember teachers and their covenants with their students, especially the main teacher, Rasulullah ﷺ Muhammad and others, such as Abraham, Moses, and Jesus

Samad: the One who does not need anything, but everyone and everything needs Allah ﷻ

Satan: the Devil, Lucifer, mentioned in divine Qurãn such as in the Bible and the Qurãn

SAW: "Sallahu alayhi wa salllam" abbreviated as "saws" when the name of Rasulullah ﷺ Muhammad is mentioned. The expressions ﷺ or saws are expressions and phrases of blessings and peace for Rasulullah ﷺ Muhammad and other prophets such as Abraham, Moses, Jesus and others.

Scent: perfume, nice smell

Scholar: expert, especially in Sufism, the experts who practice what they teach (alim)

Scripture: sacred book or sacred text

Self: ego, identifier of a person, especially in Sufism, raw and uneducated identifier and controller of a person

Service: ethical action of doing good for others and society

Spiritual Journey: struggles of following guidelines of a mystical school

State: level, especially in Sufism, spiritual level

Struggle: efforts to achieve a goal

SubhanAllah: glorification of Allah ﷻ, a divine phrase of chanting of spirituality implying a spiritual charge and discharge

SubhanAllahu wa bihamdihi: a divine phrase of glorification of Allah ﷻ

SubhanAllahul Azeem: a divine phrase of glorification of Allah ﷻ in the prostration posture

SubhanRabbiyalAzim: phrase of glorification for Allah ﷻ in the bowing posture

Submission: natural acceptance of the uncontrolled and unseen

Sufi: follower of Sufism

Sufism: mystical path of Islam

Superstitious: fake

Surrender: involuntary state of acceptance of the uncontrolled and the unseen

SWT: Subhānahu wa Tā'la also abbreviated as SWT and written as also Allah (ﷻ) is an expression of respect when the Name of Allah is mentioned.

Tahajjud: night prayer

Talismanic: unknown and indescribable effects of divine words and sounds

Taqwa: respect of Allah ﷻ

Taste: pleasure, especially spiritual pleasure such as peace, calmness, joy, and happiness in Sufism

Temple: worship place

Temporal: ending

Temporary: transitory

Temptation: false ideas

The Curer: Allah ﷻ

The Divine: Allah ﷻ

The Forgiver: a name of Allah ﷻ in Sufism

The Friend: a name of Allah ﷻ in Sufism

The Helper: a name of Allah ﷻ in Sufism

The Lover: a name of Allah ﷻ in Sufism

The Peace Giver: Allah ﷻ

The Prophet: Muhammad, Rasulullah ﷺ of Islam, referred as "the Prophet" in the text

The Real: Allah ﷻ

The Real Maker: Allah ﷻ

The Source: Allah ﷻ

The Sustainer: a name of Allah ﷻ in Sufism

The Reminder: the Qurān

The Wise: with capital W, Allah ﷻ

Throne: a figurative or metaphorical representation of dominion of Allah ﷻ

Trait: permanent character or nature

Tranquility: peace and calmness

Transcendent: beyond human limits

Transitory: temporal

Transliteration: writing the sounds of words or phrases in one language with an alphabet of another language

Union: being together, especially in this book, goal and joy of being always in the presence of Allah ﷻ

Unseen: anything five senses cannot testify in scientific methods

Weak: not having a physical strength to perform an action, especially in Sufism, not having spiritual strength to perform any action

Worshipper: a person who regularly follows and practices rituals, acts of prayers

ACKNOWLEDGMENTS

I would like to thank all my unnamed teachers, friends, and students for their input, ideas, suggestions, help, and support during and before the preparation of this book.

I would like to thank Dr. David Banks, faculty of the Department of Anthropology, State University of New York (SUNY), Sister Toni Hajdaj, Sister Umm Aisha, Dr. AbdulAhad, Br. Ali Rifat and His wife Sister Yildiz at-Turki, Sheikh Dr. Omar of Maryland al-Hindi, Sheikh Tamer of Buffalo, and Sheikh Ali of Hartford Seminary, Sisters Asya Hamad, Amina Osman, and Fatima Samrodia of Darul-Ulum Madania of Buffalo for all their editing, suggestions and comments.

I want to also thank the team of Medina House Publishing in all their preparations and efforts at all stages of this book especially Br. Murat, Br. Khalid (Halit), Br. Mehmet (Matt), Sister Karen, Sister Dorothy-Damla, and Sister Anna Engle.

Lastly, I would like to thank all of my family members for their patience with me during the preparation of this book.

We ask Allah ﷻ to accept all our efforts with the Divine Karam, Fadl, and Grace but not with our faulty and limited efforts deeming rejection. اللَّهُمَّ صلِّ عَلى سَيِّدِناَ وَ حَبِيْبَنَا وَ مَوْلَاناَ مُحَمَّد.

AUTHOR BIO

Dr. M. Yunus Kumek is currently teaching on Muslim Ministry and Spiritual Care at Harvard Divinity School. He has been religious studies coordinator at State University of New York (SUNY) Buffalo State and teaching undergraduate and graduate courses in religious studies at SUNY at Buffalo State, Niagara University and Daemen College. Before becoming interested in religious studies, Dr. Kumek was doing his doctorate degree in physics at SUNY at Buffalo, and had published academic papers in the areas of quantum physics and medical physics. Then, he decided to engage with the world of social sciences through social anthropology, education, and cultural anthropology in his doctorate studies and subsequently, spent a few years as a research associate in the anthropology department of the same university. Recently, he completed a postdoctoral fellowship at Harvard Divinity school and published books on religious literacy through ethnography and selected passages from the Quran with interpreted contextual meanings. Dr. Kumek had classical training in Islamic sciences from the teachers of Egypt, India, Turkey, Yemen, Somalia, Morocco, and the United States. He stayed and studied in Egypt and Turkey. Dr. Kumek, who remains interested in physics—solves physics problems to relax—enjoys different languages: German, Spanish, Arabic, Urdu, and Turkish, especially in his research of scriptural analysis. Dr. Kumek takes great pleasure in classical poetry as well.

SUGGESTED READINGS

Al-Ghazali, M. *Deliverance from Error*. Fons Vitae, 2000.

Al-Ghazali, M. *Ihya 'Ulum al-Din.'* Dar al-Fikr, 2004.

Al-Ghazzali, M. *On the Treatment of Anger, Hatred and Envy*. Kazi Publications, 2003.

Al-Ghazzali, M. *The Alchemy of Happiness*. Routledge, 2015.

Ali, A. Y. *The Meaning of the Glorious Qurān*. Islamic Books, 1938.

Anjum, Z. Iqbal: *The Life of a Poet, Philosopher, and Politician*. Random House, 2015.

Arberry, A. *Interpretation of Koran*. Macmillan, 1955.

Arberry. *Muslim Saints and Mystics: Episodes from Tadhirat al awliya of Faird al-Din Attar, Omphaloskepsis*, 2000.

Asad, M. *The Message of the Qurān: Translated and Explained*. Al-Andalus Gibraltar, 1980.

Avery, K. S. *A Psychology of Early Sufi Sama: Listening and Altered States*. Routledge, 2004.

Awang, R. "Anger Management: A Psychotherapy Sufistic Approach," vol. 9, no. 1, 2014, pp. 13–15.

Barks, C. *Rumi: Bridge to the Soul*. Harperone, 2007.

Barks, R. N. C. with J. Moyne, Rumi, Jelaluddin. "The guest house." *The Essential Rumi*. Harper, 1995, p. 109.

Bayrak, T. *The Name & the Named*. Canada, 2000.

Berguno, G. & Loutfy, N. "The Existential Thoughts of the Sufis. Existential Analysis." *Journal of the Society for Existential Analysis*, vol. 16, no. 1, 2005.

Bowen, J. *A New Anthropology of Islam*. Cambridge University Press, 2012.

Clarke, M. "Cough Sweets and Angels: The Ordinary Ethics of the Extraordinary in Sufi Practice in Lebanon." *Journal of the Royal Anthropological Institute*, vol. 20, no. 3, 2014, pp. 407–25.

Cutsinger, J. S. *Paths to the Heart*. World Wisdom, 2010.

Douglas-Klotz, N. *The Sufi Book of Life: 99 Pathways of the Heart for the Modern Dervish*. Penguin, 2005.

Ernst, C. W. *Teachings of Sufism*. Shambhala Publications, 1999.

Esposito, J. *The Oxford Dictionary of Islam*. Oxford University Press, 2014.

Friedlander, S. *The Whirling Dervishes: Being an Account of the Sufi Order Known as the Mevlevis and its Founder the Poet and Mystic Mevlana Jalalu'ddin Rumi*. SUNY Press, 1975.

Geoffroy, E. *Introduction to Sufism: The Inner Path of Islam*. World Wisdom, Inc., 2010.

Gibran, K. *The Prophet*. Oneworld Publications, 2012.

Hanson, Y. H. "The Creed of Imam Al-Tahawi." Zaytuna Institute, California, 2007.

Hanson, Y. H. *Purification of the Heart*. Alhambra Productions, 1998.

Helminski, K. *The Knowing Heart: A Sufi Path of Transformation*. Shambhala Publications, 2000.

Izutsu, T. *Sufism and Taoism: A Comparative Study of Key Philosophical Concepts*. University of California Press, 2016.

James, W. "The Will to Believe." *New World*, 1896.

Jawziyyah, Q. *The Prophetic Medical Science*. Idara Impex, 2013.

Karamustafa, T. A. *Sufism*. Edinburgh University Press, 2007.

Katz, J. G. "Dreams, Sufism, and Sainthood." *Brill*, vol. 71, 1996.

Khan, Z. M. *Gardens of the Righteous*. Routledge, 2012.

Lewis, B. *Music of a Distant Drum: Classical Arabic, Persian, Turkish, and Hebrew Poems*. Princeton University Press, 2001.

Malak, A. *Muslim Narratives and the Discourse of English*. SUNY Press, 2007.

Morris, J. W. "Introducing Ibn 'Arabī's Book of Spiritual Advice." *Journal of the Muhyiddīn Ibn 'Arabī Society*, no. 28, 2000, pp. 1–17.

Pickthall, M. W. E. *Holy Qurān*. Kutub Khana Isha'at-ul-Islam, 1977.

Ramji, R. *The Global Migration of Sufi Islam to South Asia and Beyond*. Brill, 2007, pp. 473–84.

Renard J. *Knowledge of Allah ﷻ in Classical Sufism: Foundations of Islamic Mystical Theology*. Paulist Press, 2004.

Rumi, J. *The Essential Rumi*. Harper, 1996.

Schimmel, A. *Deciphering the Signs of Allah ﷻ: A Phenomenological Approach to Islam.* State University of New York Press, 1994.

Siddiqui, A. "Sahih Muslim." *Peace Vision,* 1972.

Trimingham, J. S. *The Sufi Orders in Islam.* Oxford University Press, 1998.

Upton, C. *Doorkeeper of the Heart: Versions of Rabi'a.* Threshold Books, 1988.

Usmani, T. *An Approach to the Qur'anic Sciences.* Adam Publishers, 2006.

INDEX

www.ingramcontent.com/pod-product-compliance
Lightning Source LLC
Chambersburg PA
CBHW051001060726

47593CB00018B/2075